# PLATO
# MENO

D1519407

## The Focus Philosophical Library

Aristotle • De Anima • M. Shiffman

Aristotle • Nicomachean Ethics • J. Sachs

Aristotle • Poetics • J. Sachs

Aristotle • Politics • J. Sachs

Athenian Funeral Orations • J. Herrman

Descartes • Discourse on Method • R. Kennington

Empire and the Ends of Politics (Plato/Pericles) • S. D. Collins and D. Stauffer

Four Island Utopias (Plato, Euhemeros, Iambolous, Bacon) • D. Clay and A. Purvis

Hegel • The Philosophy of Right • A. White

Lucretius • On the Nature of Things • W. Englert

Plato and Xenophon • Apologies • M. Kremer

Plato • Euthydemus • M. Nichols

Plato • Gorgias • J. Arieti and R. Barrus

Plato, Gorgias • Aristotle, Rhetoric • J. Sachs

Plato • Meno • G. Anastaplo and L. Berns

Plato • Parmenides • A. K. Whitaker

Plato • Phaedo • E. Brann, P. Kalkavage, and E. Salem

Plato • Phaedrus • S. Scully

Plato • Republic • J. Sachs

Plato • Sophist • E. Brann, P. Kalkavage, and E. Salem

Plato • Statesman • E. Brann, P. Kalkavage, and E. Salem

Plato • Symposium • E. Brann, P. Kalkavage, and E. Salem

Plato • Symposium • A. Sharon

Plato • Theaetetus • J. Sachs

Plato • Timaeus, Second Edition • P. Kalkavage

Socrates and Alcibiades • Four Texts • D. Johnson

Socrates and the Sophists • J. Sachs

Spinoza: Theologico-Political Treatise • M. Yaffe

# PLATO
# MENO

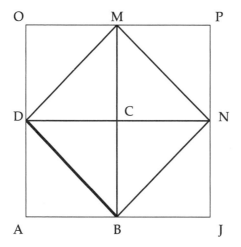

Translation, Introduction, and Glossary by
Eva Brann, Peter Kalkavage, and Eric Salem

*focus* an imprint of
Hackett Publishing Company, Inc.
Indianapolis/Cambridge

A Focus book

*Focus* *an imprint of*
Hackett Publishing Company

24 23 22 21      1 2 3 4 5 6 7

For further information, please address
        Hackett Publishing Company, Inc.
        P.O. Box 44937
        Indianapolis, Indiana 46244-0937

        www.hackettpublishing.com

Composition by Aptara, Inc.

Library of Congress Control Number: 2021934329

ISBN-13: 978-1-58510-993-7 (pbk.)
ISBN-13: 978-1-58510-995-1 (PDF ebook)

The paper used in this publication meets the minimum requirements of American National Standard for Information Sciences—Permanence of Paper for Printed Library Materials, ANSI Z39.48–1984.

∞

to St. John's College
and its spirit of shared inquiry

# CONTENTS

# INTRODUCTION

The *Meno* holds a special place among the Platonic dialogues. It is the best introduction to Plato and provides a foundation for understanding the dialogues as a whole.

Though not a long work (only thirty pages), the *Meno* is about many things. Its central topic is virtue. The Greek word for "virtue," *aretê*, means excellence and can refer to the good condition of anything, including inanimate objects. In the *Meno*, *aretê* is human excellence—the goodness that is proper to us as human beings. Meno, a young aristocrat from Thessaly, starts the dialogue by asking Socrates whether he can tell him how virtue is acquired. Very soon, however, the discussion becomes a search for what virtue *is*. The inquiry leads in turn to inquiry itself—its nature and its very possibility.

But there is more. The *Meno* makes us think about wisdom and the reputation for wisdom, teachers and students, fathers and sons, masters and slaves, the goodness of perplexity and the knowledge of one's ignorance, memory and recollection, knowledge and opinion, thought and action, political virtue and political orthodoxy. One subject in particular plays a key role in the dialogue: geometry. What does this mathematical science, we wonder, have to do with virtue and the search for what virtue is?

At the center of the work stands the man from whom the dialogue takes its title: Meno, whose name in Greek—*Menôn*—means "remaining" or "staying put." To be sure, the *Meno* is "about virtue," to quote the subtitle that may have been added later by the Hellenistic editor Thrasylus. But at a deeper level it is about Meno himself, who is the true concern and subject of the drama; and the entire conversation, as Socrates repeatedly stresses, is for Meno's sake—for his betterment. Who, then, is Meno, and why should he interest us?

Xenophon, Plato's contemporary and a fellow student of Socrates, gives a memorably scathing account of the historical Meno in his book *Anabasis*. Meno was one of the generals chosen by Aristippus, a fellow

Thessalian aristocrat, to give military aid to Cyrus, the upstart contender for the Persian crown, in the famous March of the Ten Thousand. Xenophon describes Meno as an outright scoundrel: self-interested, treacherous, and above all greedy. It is nothing short of brilliant on Plato's part to show us such a man asking (of all things!) how virtue is acquired. Plato's Meno seems indeed to be inordinately concerned with power, honor, and wealth. Socrates teasingly refers to him as good-looking, spoiled, deceptive, and tyrannical. By conventional standards, he is well educated: he knows his poets and scientists and is cozy with the technical side of mathematics. A devotee of the famous rhetorician Gorgias, whose spirit haunts the dialogue, Meno is also full of himself, proud of his ability to give many speeches about virtue on many occasions before many people.

One thing above all defines the Platonic Meno: his resistance to learning through searching. This is what makes Meno enduringly interesting to us and a touchstone of sorts. He is the exemplar of the facile, knowledge-greedy anti-learner—an avid collector of shiny opinions, who in spite of his stubbornness is willing to be led by Socrates, at least up to a point. In judging Meno, we should bear in mind that there is undoubtedly a bit of Meno in all of us, an all-too-human tendency to resist learning and to fall back on presumed knowledge and well-worn opinions, often inherited from various teachers.

The dialogue probably takes place in 402 BCE, three years before Socrates's trial and execution. At the time, Meno would have been a very young man—eighteen or nineteen. We are not told why he is in town. In light of his family's friendly ties to Athens, he may have been sent by his fellow Aleuadae, the leading clan in Larissa (the capital of Thessaly), to persuade democratic Athens to give military aid to the Thessalian aristocrats, whose hegemony had recently been threatened by the tyrant Lycophron. Meno is no doubt staying with his guest-friend Anytus, who appears later in the dialogue and who only three years later became one of Socrates's accusers at his trial for impiety and corrupting the young. It's not clear where the conversation is taking place. It might be in a gymnasium. That would fit Socrates's repeated efforts to get luxurious Meno to exert himself and break a mental sweat.

In addition to being rich in themes, the *Meno* is a good example of the Platonic dialogue as drama—that is, a work in which speeches are also deeds. Things *happen* in the *Meno*, as they do in all the dialogues, and the reader must attend carefully to these happenings, as well as to the content and flow of the argument. Meno's opening question about how virtue is acquired is the drama's first deed, as Meno tries to acquire some pearl of wisdom from the famous Socrates without having to pay for it.

In what might be called act 1 of Plato's drama (70A–79E), Meno, at Socrates's insistence, makes several attempts to say *what* virtue is, as opposed to *what sort* of thing it is—and fails each time. Why do his attempts fail? Why is Meno unable to keep virtue, as Socrates says, "whole and healthy"? What do Meno's answers reveal about who Meno is? What constitutes a "good" definition of virtue or a "good" definition of anything? What is the good of having a definition of virtue or of searching for one? How are we made better (if we are), and what do we come to realize by engaging in such a search—even, perhaps especially, when our efforts fail? These are just a few of the questions that this opening stretch of the drama raises.

If act 2 of the *Meno* (80A–86C) had a title, it would be "In Defense of Learning." Frustrated by his failed attempts, Meno compares snub-nosed, bulgy-eyed Socrates to a numbfish or stingray that has stunned Meno into speechless torpor—not a condition Meno is used to. The image reveals Meno's wit and his stunted view of perplexity. Perplexity—in Greek, *aporia*—is one of the dialogue's central terms. It means "impasse" but refers more broadly to the condition of being without a *poros*—a "means," "resource," or "provision." For Meno, who prides himself on his wealth of ready-to-mouth speeches, *aporia* is a dead stop. For Socrates, it is the enlivening source and begetter of philosophic desire—an energizing form of poverty, a poverty that enriches.

In the dialogue's most crucial turning point, Meno tries to numb Socrates in return. He does so with a clever paradox he no doubt picked up from Gorgias. Like the philosopher Zeno's famous paradox of the arrow that cannot fly (because at each moment it stands still in the very place it is), Meno's paradox is an attempt to kill motion—the motion of learning and searching. The argument goes like this. If you don't know what you're searching for, you won't know it—recognize it—when you meet it; and if you do know it, then there's no need to search. In either case, there is no intellectual motion: no searching and learning.

Instead of trying to untangle Meno's Gorgian knot, Socrates cuts it—with a myth. According to the myth Socrates tells, the soul is deathless and through her countless rebirths has seen the eternal order of things, the interconnected whole of nature. Learning, then, is not the acquisition of knowledge but the summoning up or recollection (*anamêsis*) of "past" knowledge. The myth's temporal language invites us to search for the nontemporal meaning that is no doubt implied. We get a glimpse of this timeless meaning later in the dialogue when Socrates calls recollection a "reasoning out of the cause." To "go back" is to proceed in one's thinking from a given truth that is merely opined to the source and ground of that truth. The soul can search and learn because she has an eternal, timeless bond with eternal, timeless truth, and because opinions, even false ones, are the glimmerings and traces of insights yet to be recovered.

What the myth asserts is shockingly unconventional—that learning is not the result of teaching, not a transport of knowledge from one human vessel that is "full" to another that is "empty." A slave to his habit of intellectual passivity, Meno asks Socrates to *teach* him the truth of the myth. No, Socrates can't do that, he says; but he can *show* Meno an instance of learning as recollection. He does so by taking one of Meno's many slaves through a geometrical problem: the doubling of a square. A question, then, naturally arises: how does this effort at geometric doubling serve as a paradigm in the search for what virtue is?

The problem is interesting for many reasons, more than can be mentioned here. The most obvious is that the problem involves an image— a figure drawn in the sand. Thanks to the image, the conversation will have a visual referent: Socrates and the slave-boy will have something to look at in the course of their speech, something out in the open that will guide speech and keep it honest. Gorgian wordplay is out of the question here. Moreover, the image is something not just to be looked at but to be engaged with: the search will involve the drawing of lines and the actual construction of the sought-for square. Readers of the *Meno* are here called upon to share in this construction, or rather in the step-by-step process by which the *side* of the double square is made to appear—a magnitude that can be seen and shown but not "said."

The slave-boy episode—the dialogue's marvelous play within a play—dramatizes a genuine act of learning. Unlike his master, Meno's slave-boy attends fully to the matter at hand, unimpeded by vanity, sophistication, and the presumption of intellectual wealth. He follows Socrates's lead astutely, follows the argument wherever it goes, and, in striking contrast to Meno, frankly admits his errors and perplexity. In this one act of learning and intelligent following, the slave-boy shows himself to be far freer than his master, freer in mind and soul.

The display of learning as recollection is meant for Meno's sake and, by extension, for ours. Its purpose is not to explain learning—in Greek, *mathêsis*—but to rescue it from Meno's attempted mathecide. It is also meant to persuade Meno, even inspire him, to keep searching for what virtue is and to cultivate courage and endurance, virtues that searching requires. But in spite of what he has witnessed and momentarily admires Meno resists. True to his name, Staying-Put, he reverts to his original question and asks once more about how virtue is acquired, about *what sort o* thing virtue is, its attributes, even though he has not yet discovered *wha* it is. What can one do with such a person, for whom freedom, as Socrate makes clear, means playing the master in all things and rejecting any limi to his desires?

Rather than give up, Socrates suggests a *modus vivendi* that lead to the third and final act of Plato's drama (86D–100B)—a "hypothesis,

Socrates calls it, like the ones geometers sometimes use in their inquiries. The hypothesis connects Meno's obsession with how virtue is acquired to Socrates's emphasis on searching for what virtue is. The hypothesis is: "virtue is knowledge." If this could be shown to be true, Socrates asserts, then virtue would be teachable. Of course, the assumption that knowledge is teachable contradicts the myth's assertion that there is no teaching, only the learner's recollection. Why, then, does Socrates pursue this line of inquiry? What does he hope to reveal?

This final stretch of the dialogue is complex, to say the least. In its first part (86D–89C), Socrates gets Meno to conclude that virtue is, after all, a form of knowledge. Socrates calls this knowledge *phronêsis*, or "thoughtfulness," the wisdom that guides the proper use of virtues like courage and moderation and even material things like wealth. When this intelligent, statesmanlike virtue is present, then all such things, whether of soul or of body, are good and helpful; and when it is not, then bad and harmful. At this point in the dialogue, we seem to have reached something altogether positive.

This promising view is unfortunately short-lived, as Socrates himself undercuts it with a surprising question: if virtue is indeed a form of knowledge, and if knowledge is teachable, then where are its teachers? The question continues the dialogue's "descent" into the realm of *doxa*, which in Greek means both "opinion" and "good repute." The descent began when Meno's stubbornness (his desire to be free) forced Socrates to abandon the quest for what virtue is in order to search for how virtue might be acquired.

Enter Anytus. He may have been hovering somewhere nearby and only now joins Meno, his guest-friend, and Socrates. He appears suddenly, seemingly out of nowhere. Socrates treats him like a gift from above, a divine being who has arrived just in time to help mere mortals in their present crisis. Socrates lays special emphasis on the virtues of Anytus's father, a diligent businessman and well-mannered citizen who saw to it that his son had a good education. The implication seems to be that virtue can indeed be passed from father to son (if, that is, the son really is virtuous). Whom should Meno consult, Socrates asks, if he wants not merely to have an answer to the question about how virtue is acquired but to become virtuous? Anytus gives the answer that Socrates surely expects from his fellow Athenian: Meno should take as his model and teacher any of the good and fine men of the city, those who are widely reputed to be virtuous.

The conversation with Anytus is the second play within a play that is staged, it would seem, for Meno's benefit. The first was the slave-boy episode. There, Meno witnessed an act of successful (if limited) learning. In the Anytus episode, he witnesses the uncompromising rejection of all things intellectual and the closed-minded defense of Athenian public figures like Themistocles and Pericles. Meno also gets to see on display the political counterpart and inverse of his own resistance to learning. Whereas Meno lets any opinion into his soul, so long as it is impressive sounding, and resists the work and risk of learning, Anytus vehemently sticks to one opinion—that of the city. And whereas Meno is blithely open to the views of sophists, Anytus, without having any acquaintance with sophists whatsoever, verbally attacks these men as dangerous intellectuals who undermine public opinion and public virtue. If Meno is in fact staying at the house of Anytus, as he probably is, one wonders what sort of conversation they had after their talk with Socrates!

In Socrates's blunt, not to say brazen, interrogation of Anytus (who did not seem hostile to Socrates when he entered the conversation), Plato dramatizes the origin and cause of the indictment brought against Socrates, or at least one aspect of it, since we learn in the *Apology* that Anytus was angry with Socrates for his condemnation of Athenian politicians. Here in the *Meno*, Socrates's act of putting Anytus on trial, as it were, not only incites the man's defensiveness on behalf of these political icons but also raises a question: if these men were indeed virtuous and led their cities well, why didn't they, as good fathers, pass on this virtue to their sons, as Anytus is compelled to admit? There can only be one reason, Socrates concludes: virtue is not something teachable. At this point, Anytus, the self-proclaimed watchdog of the city, has had enough and issues his ominous warning before leaving the conversation: if Socrates persists in bad-mouthing esteemed political figures, he will suffer the city's wrath—as indeed he does.

In what immediately follows, Socrates gets Meno to agree that nobody thinks that virtue is teachable. Meno's beloved Gorgias certainly doesn't think it is and even ridicules other sophists for holding that opinion. And poets like Theognis contradict themselves on the matter. The conclusion seems evident: there are no teachers of virtue and, Socrates significantly adds, no learners either.

The admission brings us to the last part of this third and final act of the *Meno*, as Socrates proposes that "correct opinion" is just as good a guide as knowledge in matters of action, a view that echoes in part the position of Anytus. Someone, for example, who has never been to Larissa but nevertheless has a correct opinion about how to get there would be just as good a guide as someone who traveled along the road and knew it from experience. What, then, is the difference between "knowledge" and "correct opinion," and why is the former held in higher esteem than the latter?

To answer these questions, Socrates appeals to recollection, which had been displaced by teaching in this third act of Plato's drama. To know is to bind correct opinions, which otherwise tend to flee from us, with recollection as a "reasoning out of the cause." To clarify his point, Socrates uses two striking images: the statues of the famed craftsman Daedalus, which were said to be so lifelike that they moved around, and runaway slaves. Unfettered correct opinions are like both. The images are perplexing. In what sense is knowledge like a tied-down statue and a fettered slave? This much is clear: Socrates has chosen images that are tailored to Meno's acquisitive streak and desire for mastery. (Statue and slave in fact recall two of Meno's earlier definitions, according to which virtue was the possession of beautiful things and rule over others.) What collector would want a valuable item that could be acquired but not reliably possessed? What master would want a slave who was always on the verge of turning fugitive? Perhaps the deeper question at work here is this: what does it mean for a true thing to be genuinely and lastingly one's own?

So how is virtue—here, understood as the virtue of guiding a city well—acquired? Socrates goes through the candidates in Meno's opening question one by one, and by what seems like an all too quick process of elimination reaches the following conclusion: political virtue, when it comes, must come from some *theia moira*, some divine allotment and inspiration. The famous statesmen whom Anytus defended are therefore at the same level as soothsayers and prophets who utter many true things, but without knowing of what they speak. How Anytus—who it seems still hovers nearby—would respond to *that* is not hard to imagine.

It is important to note that the identification of virtue with thoughtfulness has not been refuted by this argument but only put to one side. It is Socrates's dubious conjoining of "knowledge" and "teachableness" that seems to undermine that earlier claim. There still remains the possibility that virtue is thoughtfulness, and that this can be learned, or at least cultivated, without being teachable in the way that, say, horsemanship is teachable.

The drama ends in the Underworld. If there were someone who could teach political virtue to another, he would be like Tiresias in the *Odyssey*—a true thing among flitting shades. The reason is that he, like Tiresias, would have his wits about him and be capable of speech. But is not Tiresias, too, an inspired prophet, one who utters true things without knowing why they are true? In any case, the negative conclusions reached in the third act are merely provisional and are themselves "shady," depending as they do on the hypothesis-based inquiry into *what sort* of thing virtue is. The solid truth will come to light, Socrates pointedly tells Meno, only through a return to the search for *what* virtue is, the search that Meno resists.

In the closing lines of the dialogue, Socrates sends Meno on a political mission. If Meno could persuade his host of the things of which he himself has been persuaded—perhaps the goodness and importance of conversation—he would make Anytus gentler, presumably toward Socrates and his commitment to shared searching. Meno, an aristocratic foreigner, would thereby confer no small benefit on democratic Athens. Would the Meno we have come to know be willing to do such a thing? It seems unlikely. Would Anytus be open to persuasion? The *Apology* is the answer to that question.

*

Our goal in translating the *Meno* was the same as that of our previous efforts: to remain as faithful as possible to the Greek while using lively, colloquial English. In preparing this edition, we used the Oxford text edited by John Burnet. We regularly consulted various translations. Especially helpful were those by George Anastaplo and Laurence Berns, Robert C. Bartlett, G. M. A. Grube, and the German translation by Friedrich Schleiermacher. We also consulted the critical editions and notes by E. S. Thompson, R. S. Bluck, Richard McKirahan, and W. J. Verdenius. We acknowledge, in addition, our indebtedness to Jacob Klein's *A Commentary on Plato's Meno*.

We wish to thank all those who reviewed drafts of the translation and offered their generous support for our project. We are especially indebted to two St. John's graduates, Timothy Creighton and Catherine Halter, for their perceptive comments and suggestions.

An enormous debt of thanks must go to Keith Whitaker, whose keen eye for detail, knowledge of Greek, and understanding of Plato helped make this edition more fully what it was meant to be.

Finally, we wish to thank our friend and colleague Jennifer Behrens, who produced the geometrical diagrams that appear in the translation.

And now . . . let the drama begin!

PETER KALKAVAGE
FALL 2020

# MENO

### Meno, Socrates, Meno's slave-boy, Anytus

70A **Meno:** Can you tell me, Socrates, whether virtue is something teachable?[1] Or not teachable but attainable through practice? Or is it neither attainable through practice nor learnable, but instead comes to human beings by nature or in some other way?

**Socrates:** Meno, before this the Thessalians were well thought of among the Greeks and were admired for both horsemanship

B and wealth, but now, as it seems to me, also for wisdom, and not least the Larissaeans, fellow citizens of your comrade Aristippus. And the one responsible for this for you all is Gorgias. For having arrived in the city, he captured as lovers for wisdom the leading men of the Aleuadae, among whom is your lover Aristippus and those of the rest of the Thessalians as well.[2] And in particular—inasmuch as he himself even offers himself to anyone among the Greeks who wants to ask whatever he wants, and fails to answer no one at all—he has habituated you all to this habit, namely, to answer fearlessly and magnificently whenever someone asks something, as is fitting for those who know. But

C here, my dear Meno, the opposite has come about. For it's as if

---

1  *didakton*—either "teachable" or "taught." The Greek words for "attainable through practice" (*askêton*) and "learnable" (*mathêton*) are similarly ambiguous.

2  Socrates makes many historical references in his initial response to Meno. He names names—places, individuals, and groups. Larissa was the major city in Thessaly, a district in northern Greece. In the *Crito*, Socrates describes Thessaly as a place where there is "much disorder and incontinence" (53D). The Aleuadae were the hereditary ruling family in Larissa. Aristippus, a prominent member of that family, gave military aid to Cyrus in his effort to wrest the Persian throne from his brother (the famous March of the Ten Thousand). He appointed Meno as one of the generals of his mercenaries, apparently under the spell of Meno's youthful beauty (Xenophon, *Anabasis* 2.6.28). Gorgias of Leontini was the most famous teacher of rhetoric in all of Greece. He appears in the dialogue that bears his name.

71A  some wisdom-drought has occurred, and I'm afraid wisdom has emigrated from these places here to where you all live. At any rate, if you're willing to ask one of our people here about this, there's no one who won't laugh and say: "Stranger, I'm afraid I seem to you to be someone blessed—to know, that is, whether virtue is something teachable or in whatever way it comes to us. But I'm so far from knowing whether it's something teachable or not teachable that I don't even happen to know *it*—what in the world this thing virtue is—at all."

B    Now I myself, Meno, am also in this condition. I'm poverty-stricken in this matter along with my fellow citizens, and I blame myself for not knowing about virtue at all. And if I don't know *what* something is, how would I know *what sort* of thing it is? Or does it seem to you to be possible that someone who doesn't know[3] Meno at all, who he is, could know[4] whether he's beautiful or rich and also well-born, or even the opposite of these? Does it seem to you to be possible?

C    **Meno:** Not to me. But you, Socrates—do you truly not know what virtue is, and is this the report we're to spread about you even back home?

**Socrates:** Not only that, my comrade, but also that I never ran into anyone else who knew, as it seems to me.

**Meno:** What? Didn't you run into Gorgias when he was here?

**Socrates:** I did indeed.

**Meno:** Really? He didn't seem to you to know?

**Socrates:** I'm not one to remember very well,[5] Meno, so I can't say at the present how he seemed to me at that time. But perhaps he

D    does know, and you know what he said. Remind[6] me, then, how

---

3  *gignôskei*—"know" in the sense of "be familiar with" or "recognize."

4  *eidenai*—"know" in the sense of "know about" or "know that something is true."

5  *mnêmôn*—"good at remembering." The word resembles Meno's name in Greek: *Menôn*, which means "remaining," "not budging," "staying put" (from *menein*, which appears at 87D), so Socrates plays on Meno's name here: "It doesn't stick in my mind, O Stickler."

6  *anamnêson*—from *anamimnêskein*, "to remind," also "to recall" or "to recollect." This is the first appearance in the dialogue of a word related to *anamnêsis*, "recollection."

he spoke. But if you prefer, tell me yourself, for I'm sure things seem to you just as they do to him.

**Meno:** To me they do indeed.

**Socrates:** Well then, let's let him be, since in fact he's not here. But you yourself, Meno—by the gods, what do you claim virtue is? Tell me and don't be grudging, in order that I might have lied the luckiest lie, if it should become apparent that you and Gorgias know, whereas I said I'd never yet run into anybody who knew.

E     **Meno:** But Socrates, it's not hard to say. First, if you want a man's virtue, it's very easy. *This* is a man's virtue: to be competent to mind the city's business, and in so doing to do well by his friends and harm to his enemies,[7] and to be careful himself not to suffer anything of that sort. And if you want a woman's virtue, it's not hard to go through: she must manage her house well, both keeping safe what's inside and being obedient to her husband.[8] And there's another virtue for a child, both female and male, and for an older man, and, if you want, for a free man, and, if you want,

72A   for a slave. And there are a great many other virtues, so that there's no perplexity,[9] regarding virtue, in saying what it is. For in accordance with each of our actions and ages, with respect to each function for each of us, there's a virtue—and in the same way, I think, Socrates, also a vice.

**Socrates:** I seem to have come into possession of some great good fortune, Meno, if in searching for one virtue I've discovered

B     a sort of swarm of virtues set beside you.[10] And yet, Meno, in keeping with this likeness of swarms, if I were to ask you about the being[11] of a bee, what in the world it is, and you were to assert that they were many and varied, what would you answer

---

7    One of several definitions of justice put forth in book 1 of the *Republic* and refuted by Socrates (334B). In book 4, Socrates defines justice as "minding *one's own* business."

8    The word for "husband" is *anêr*, which is also the word for "man" (above).

9    *aporia*—"impasse," or "lack of means or resources." For Socrates, the admission of perplexity is an admirable sign of the willingness to learn.

10   Socrates uses the likeness of a swarm in the *Republic* (a swarm of arguments at 450B and a swarm of pleasures at 574D).

11   *ousias.* The word *ousia* here refers to the being itself, the very being, of something. It foreshadows the form or *eidos*, which Socrates soon mentions (72C).

me, if I asked you: "Are you claiming that they are many and varied and differ from one another in this, in being bees? Or do they not differ at all in this, but in something else, for example, in beauty or size or some other such thing?" Tell me: what would you answer, if you were asked in this way?

**Meno:** I, for one, would say this—that they don't differ at all, one from the other, insofar as they're bees.

C   **Socrates:** Then if, after this, I said, "Well then, tell me just this, Meno. The respect in which they in no way differ but are all the same thing—what do you claim this is?" No doubt you could tell me something?[12]

**Meno:** I certainly could.

**Socrates:** Well, it's like that concerning the virtues, too: even if they are many and varied, they all have at least one thing, a form,[13] that's the same, through which they're virtues, and which the one answering would do well, I suppose, to look off toward,[14]

D   to make clear to the one who asked him that very thing, namely, what virtue happens to be. Or don't you understand what I'm saying?

**Meno:** To myself I seem to understand. Still, I don't yet have down what's being asked, at least not as I want to.

**Socrates:** Does it seem to you that way only about virtue, Meno—that there's one for a man, another for a woman and for the rest—or is it the same concerning health and size and strength? Does it seem to you that there's one health for a man, another for a woman? Or is it the same form everywhere, if in fact there is

E   health, whether it's in a man or in anyone else?

**Meno:** It seems to me that at least the health of both a man and of a woman is the same.

**Socrates:** Then also size and strength? Whenever a woman is strong, will she be strong by the same form and the same strength? What I mean by "the same" is this: strength doesn't differ at

---

12   Socrates mimics Meno's "Can you tell me?"

13   "Form" translates *eidos*—from the aorist or simple past for *horan*, "to see." The word can mean a visible look or an intelligible form. The related verb, *eidenai*, appeared at 71A and B.

14   *apoblepsanta*—from *apoblepein*, "to look away from all other objects in order to focus on one." Socrates uses the verb in an almost identical context in the *Euthyphro* (6E).

all in respect of its being strength, whether it's in a man or in a woman. Or does it seem to you that they differ in some way?

**Meno:** Not to me, at least.

73A **Socrates:** And will virtue differ in some way with respect to being virtue, whether it's in a child or in an elder, or in a woman or in a man?

**Meno:** To me, at least, Socrates, this case somehow no longer seems similar to those others.

**Socrates:** What about this? Weren't you asserting that a man's virtue is to manage a city well, a woman's, a household?[15]

**Meno:** I was.

**Socrates:** Then is it possible to manage a city or a household or anything else well without managing it moderately and justly?

**Meno:** Certainly not.

B **Socrates:** Then if they manage justly and moderately, they'll manage with justice and moderation?

**Meno:** That's a necessity.

**Socrates:** Both of them, woman and man, therefore need the same things, justice and moderation, if they are to be good?

**Meno:** They appear to.

**Socrates:** What about a child and an elder? Would they ever become good while being undisciplined and unjust?

**Meno:** Certainly not.

**Socrates:** But rather by being moderate and just?

C **Meno:** Yes.

**Socrates:** All human beings, therefore, are good in the same way; for by happening to get the same things they become good.

**Meno:** That's likely.

**Socrates:** No doubt if the same virtue didn't belong to them, they wouldn't be good in the same way.

**Meno:** Certainly not.

---

15 According to Meno's definition, the virtue of a man was to mind the city's business (*ta tês poleôs prattein*) and that of a woman to manage the household well (*tên oikian eu oikein*). Socrates now shifts to a house-related verb that covers both cases—*dioikein*, "manage" or "govern." The shift may suggest that a city needs to be managed like a well-run household, in which what's inside is well protected and kept in its proper place.

**Socrates:** Well then, since the same virtue belongs to all, try to say and to recollect what thing Gorgias claims it is, and you along with him.

D   **Meno:** What else but to be able to rule human beings? If, that is, you're searching for just one thing that ranges over all cases.

**Socrates:** But that's just what I'm searching for. Still, does this same virtue belong even to a child and to a slave, Meno—for the pair to be able to rule the master—and does it seem to you that he who is doing the ruling would still be a slave?

**Meno:** That doesn't seem to me to be at all the case, Socrates.

**Socrates:** No, for it's not likely, best of men. For consider this further thing, too. You say "being able to rule." Shouldn't we add right here "justly, and not unjustly"?

**Meno:** I, at least, think so. For justice, Socrates, is virtue.

E   **Socrates:** Virtue, Meno, or a certain virtue?

**Meno:** What do you mean?

**Socrates:** As with anything else. For example, regarding roundness, if you like, I, at least, would say that it's a certain shape, not so simply that it's shape. And this is why I'd say it this way, because there are also other shapes.

**Meno:** And you'd be speaking correctly, since I, too, affirm that not only is there justice, but there are other virtues as well.

74A **Socrates:** What are they? Tell me. For example, I, too, would tell you other shapes as well, if you should order me, so you, too, tell me other virtues.

**Meno:** Well then, courage seems to me, at least, to be a virtue, and moderation and wisdom and magnificence[16] and a great many others.

**Socrates:** Once more, Meno, we've suffered the same thing: in searching for one, we've again found many virtues, though in another way than we did a little while ago; but the one virtue, which is present throughout all these, we keep not being able to discover.

---

16  The four virtues of particular interest to Socrates are justice, wisdom, moderation, and courage—the so-called "cardinal virtues" (see *Republic* 4.427E). Meno substitutes the more colorful "magnificence" for "justice." Earlier, Socrates connected magnificence with Gorgias's rhetorical style (70B).

**Meno:** For I'm not yet able, Socrates, to grasp, in the way you're

B     seeking it, one virtue that ranges over all, as in the other cases.

**Socrates:** That's quite likely. But I'll be eager to move us forward, if I'm able. For you understand, I suppose, that this holds in every case: if someone should ask you what I was saying just now— "What is shape, Meno?"—and if you told him it was roundness, and if he said to you what I did, "Is roundness shape or a certain shape?"—you'd no doubt tell him it was a certain shape.

**Meno:** Entirely so.

C  **Socrates:** Is this why, then: because there are other shapes as well?

**Meno:** Yes.

**Socrates:** And if he were to ask you further what sort they are, you'd cite them?

**Meno:** I would.

**Socrates:** And again, if he asked in the same way about color— what it is—and if you said it was white, and after that he took you up on this and asked, "Is white color or a certain color?" you'd say it's a certain color, because there happen to be others as well?

**Meno:** I would.

D    **Socrates:** And if he ordered you to cite other colors, would you cite others, which happen to be colors no less than white is?

**Meno:** Yes.

**Socrates:** If, then, he pursued the argument, just as I did, and said, "We always arrive at many, but don't put it that way for me. Rather, since you address these many by some one name, and since you claim that not a single one of them isn't shape—even those that are also opposed to each other—what is that which encompasses the round no less than the straight, which you

E     indeed name 'shape,' so that you claim that the round is no more shape than the straight?"[17] Aren't you putting it that way?

**Meno:** I am.

---

17   In other words, shape is equally present in both round and straight. Socrates here uses the language of quantity to point to something perplexing about differentiation within a given genus or "kind." Shape is somehow present as an undivided whole in each of its instances, which "participate" in shape. The problem of participation among forms is treated more extensively in other dialogues, notably the *Sophist* (251A ff.).

**Socrates:** So, when you put it that way, are you then claiming that the round is no more round than straight, or the straight no more straight than round?

**Meno:** Surely not, Socrates.

**Socrates:** And yet you're claiming that the round is no more shape than the straight, and the other way around.

**Meno:** What you say is true.

75A **Socrates:** What in the world, then, is this thing, of which the name is this: "shape"? Try to say. If, to the one asking you in this way about either shape or color, you said, "But for my part, I don't even understand what you want, mister, nor do I even know what you're saying," perhaps he'd be surprised and say, "Don't you understand that I'm searching for that which covers all these and is the same?" Or not even in the case of these examples, Meno, could you say, if someone were to ask you, "What is it that covers the round and the straight and the others, which in fact you call shapes, and is the same thing that covers them all?" Try to tell me, in order that you might also get exercise[18] for the answer about virtue.

B **Meno:** No, Socrates, but you tell me.

**Socrates:** You want me to gratify you?

**Meno:** By all means.

**Socrates:** Then will you, too, be willing to tell me about virtue?

**Meno:** I will.

**Socrates:** Well then, I must make the effort, for it's worthwhile.

**Meno:** It most certainly is.

**Socrates:** Come, then, let us try to tell you what shape is. So consider whether you would accept it to be this very thing. Let *this*, for us, be shape: that which alone among the things that *are* always happens to accompany color.[19] Is this sufficient for you,

---

18   *meletê*—also, "care" or "attention." In the *Phaedo*, Socrates defines philoso phy as the practice or care (*meletê*) of death (67E).

19   Socrates's definition rests on our ordinary perceptual experience: t perceive color is to perceive colored *surfaces*, which always appear t us as shaped in various ways. Shape always accompanies color in tha it always appears along with color, just as color always accompanie perceived shape. The two always appear together. But how might th definition serve as a model in the search for virtue? By using the ana ogy of shape and color, Socrates seems to be inviting Meno to search fc the one thing that always accompanies a given virtue so as to make

or are you somehow searching for something else? For I'd be
C    content if you would tell me about virtue in just the same way.

**Meno:** But that's so simpleminded,[20] Socrates.

**Socrates:** What do you mean?

**Meno:** That shape, according to your account, is, I take it, that
which always accompanies color.[21] All right. But if in fact someone should deny that he knows color but is perplexed about it in
the same way he was about shape, what do you think you would
have answered?[22]

**Socrates:** The truth, I think. And if the person asking me should be
one of those who are wise, with a knack for contention and strife,
D    I would tell him, "What I've said I've said. But if I'm not speaking
correctly, it's your job to take hold of the account and refute it."
But if, being friends, just as you and I now are, they should want
to converse with one another, then they must answer in a way
that's somehow gentler and more conducive to conversation.[23]
And it's perhaps more conducive to conversation to answer not
only with what's true but also by way of those things that the
one asking[24] would in addition agree he knows. Now I, too, will

---

appear in its proper "shape"—in a way that is truly good. Later in the
dialogue, this will be identified as "thoughtfulness" or *phronêsis* (88B).
As we see, Socrates's effort fails. Meno dismisses the definition as "simpleminded." It fails to satisfy his taste for things sophisticated, that is,
Gorgian.

20   *euêthes*—from *eu*, "well," and *êthos*, "character." In addition to meaning
simpleminded or naive, the word can mean "well-disposed" or "good-
natured."

21   Meno shifts from Socrates's general word for "color," *chrôma*, to *chroa*,
which can refer either to the surface of the body or to skin color or com-
plexion. Socrates picks up on the shift at 76D. The change signals an
emphasis on color as belonging to the *surface* of a thing. Meno has unwit-
tingly brought color into even closer relation with shape as a limit or
boundary.

22   Meno mimics Socrates's appeal to a hypothetical interlocutor. Some
commentators, following Meno's lead, point out that Socrates's definition is faulty because it defines an unknown in terms of something more
unknown. In fact, Meno here offers a good example of using a logical tech-
nicality as an obstruction tactic.

23   Or, "more dialectical," *dialektikôteron*. Similarly, "to converse" translates
*dialegesthai*, the verb "to dialogue," Socrates's characteristic activity.

24   Reading, with Thompson and Bluck, *erôtôn*, "asking," rather than *erôtôme-
nos*, "being asked." See E. S. Thompson, *The Meno of Plato*, rev. ed. (1901;

E    try to speak to you in this way. Tell me, do you call something an "end"? I mean some such thing as limit or extremity—by all these I mean the same thing. Prodicus[25] would perhaps differ with us, but you, at least, would no doubt call something "limited" and "ended."[26] That's the sort of thing I want to say, nothing fancy.

**Meno:** But I do call it that, and I think I understand what you're saying.

76A   **Socrates:** What about this? Do you call something a plane surface, and something else in turn a solid—those things, for example, that come up in matters of geometry?

**Meno:** Yes, I do call them that.

**Socrates:** Well then, on this basis you may now understand from me what I mean by shape. I assert, in the case of every shape, that this is shape: that in which the solid reaches its limit. To sum up, what I would say is that shape is "limit of solid."[27]

**Meno:** And what do you assert color is, Socrates?

**Socrates:** You're an arrogant one, Meno.[28] You order up problems for an elderly man to answer, but you yourself aren't
B    willing to recollect and tell me what in the world Gorgias asserts virtue is.

---

repr., New York: Garland Publishing, Inc., 1980), 239–40, and R. S. Bluck, *Plato's Meno* (Cambridge: Cambridge University Press, 1961), 246–48.

25   Prodicus of Ceos, a sophist known for making fine, not to say pedantic, verbal distinctions. Socrates later cites him (no doubt playfully) as one of his teachers (96D). In the *Theaetetus*, Socrates says that when he encounters prospective associates who are not pregnant in soul, he sends them "to Prodicus, and many to other wise and divinely inspired men" (151B).

26   The verb Socrates uses (*teteleutêkenai*), especially in the aorist or perfect (as here), can have the sense of "having come to the end of life." As opposed to Socrates's first definition, which evokes color and surface and skin, there is something lifeless, dead, about his second approach.

27   Unlike the earlier, experience-based definition of shape (75B), this technical, theory-based one, which Meno had a hand in crafting, refers to the purely geometrical "solids" found in books 11–13 of Euclid's *Elements*. See Jacob Klein, *A Commentary on Plato's Meno* (Chapel Hill: University of North Carolina Press, 1965), 65–67.

28   Socrates calls Meno a *hybristês*—someone who exhibits *hybris*, a word that suggests impiety and violence.

**Meno:** But as soon as you tell me this, Socrates, I *will* tell you.

**Socrates:** Even someone who's been blindfolded, Meno, would recognize by the way you converse that you are beautiful and still have lovers.

**Meno:** Why is that?

C

**Socrates:** Because you do nothing in discussions but give orders, the very thing that spoiled boys do, inasmuch as they play the tyrant while they're in the bloom of youth, and at the same time you perhaps recognize about me that I have a weakness for beauties. So, I'll gratify you and answer.

**Meno:** By all means. Gratify away!

**Socrates:** Then do you want me to answer you in Gorgias fashion, in a way that you would follow most easily?

**Meno:** I do want that. Of course.

**Socrates:** Then do you all speak of certain effluences from the things that *are*, in Empedocles fashion?[29]

**Meno:** Absolutely.

**Socrates:** And of openings into which and through which the effluences pass?

**Meno:** Certainly.

D

**Socrates:** And of the effluences, some fit some of the openings, while others are too little or too big?

**Meno:** That's it.

**Socrates:** Then do you also call something sight?

**Meno:** I do.

---

29  Empedocles of Acragas in Sicily—natural philosopher and poet, who taught that natural events were caused by Love and Strife among the four elements of body: Earth, Air, Fire, and Water. For Empedocles, effluences or "off-flows" (*aporrhoai*) are films that are exuded from material objects. These films consist of particles that fit the various pores in the organs of sense, as Socrates proceeds to explain. Socrates's yoking of the Gorgian and Empedoclean styles is striking. Gorgias is said to have studied with his fellow Sicilian; and Aristotle, in a fragment from a lost work, credits Empedocles with being the founder of rhetoric. See J. H. Freese, introduction to Aristotle's *Art of Rhetoric*, Loeb Classical Library (Cambridge: Harvard University Press, 1967), ix.

**Socrates:** On this basis, then, "Comprehend what I say to you," as Pindar[30] proclaimed. For color is an effluence of shapes commensurate with sight and perceptible.[31]

**Meno:** You seem to me, Socrates, to have put this answer in a most excellent way.

E **Socrates:** For perhaps it was put in a way that accords with your habit.[32] And at the same time, I think you realize that on the basis of this answer you'd be able to say what sound is, too, and smell and many other such things.

**Meno:** By all means.

**Socrates:** For the answer is high-flown,[33] Meno, and as a result it pleases you more than the one about shape.

**Meno:** It does indeed.

**Socrates:** But it's not better, child of Alexidemus—so I persuade myself—but that other one is.[34] Nor do I think it would even seem so to you, if, as you were saying yesterday,[35] it wasn't necessary for you to go away before the Mysteries,[36] but if you were to stay around and be initiated.

77A **Meno:** But I would stay around, Socrates, if you said many such things to me.

**Socrates:** Well then, I won't at all be lacking in eagerness, at least, in saying such things, both for your sake and for mine; but I fear

---

30   Greatest of the Greek lyric poets (c. 518–438 BCE). Socrates quotes the same phrase at *Phaedrus* 236D. Bluck observes that these invocations of Pindar "add to the general air of mock-profundity" (251). For an interesting discussion of the quotation in the *Meno*, see Klein, 68n40.

31   Earlier, Socrates, in his "simpleminded" way, defined shape in terms of color (75B). Now, in a fancy mode, he defines color in terms of shape.

32   It is tempting to connect Meno's habit with the fancy definition of color that just poetically emanated from Socrates. The colorful definition had exactly the right "shape" to fit the Gorgian "groove" in Meno's soul.

33   *tragikē*—"tragical" in the sense of "majestic." The word can also mean "pompous."

34   To which definition of shape is Socrates referring—the experience-based one, which Meno rejected as naive, or the technical-geometric one, which he seemed to find congenial? See Klein, 70.

35   This indicates that Socrates has already had a chance to get to know Meno and form an opinion of him.

36   The Mysteries in honor of Demeter and Persephone were held at Eleusis, a place near Athens.

I won't be able to tell you many. But come now, you, too: try to fulfill your promise to me to tell me about virtue as a whole— what it is—and stop making many out of one, as the jokers proclaim every time people break something. Instead, leaving it whole and healthy, tell me what virtue is. The models, at any

B      rate, you've gotten from me.

Meno: Well then, Socrates, it seems to me that virtue is, just as the poet says, "to rejoice in beautiful things and to be capable."[37] I, too, assert that virtue is this: for one who desires beautiful things to be capable of providing them for himself.[38]

Socrates: Do you assert that he who desires beautiful things is a desirer of good things?[39]

Meno: Yes, most definitely.

Socrates: On the assumption that there are some people who desire

C      bad things, but others good? Don't all people, best of men, seem to you to desire good things?

Meno: Not to me.

Socrates: But some, bad things?

Meno: Yes.

Socrates: Thinking that the bad things are good, you mean, or even recognizing that they're bad they desire them just the same?

Meno: Both, it seems to me.

Socrates: Really? Does someone who recognizes that bad things are bad seem to you, Meno, to desire them just the same?

Meno: Most definitely.

Socrates: What do you assert he desires? Isn't it that they become his?

D      Meno: That they become his. What else?

Socrates: Believing that bad things help him to whom they come, or recognizing that bad things harm him to whom they're present?

---

37    Perhaps from a poem by Simonides of Ceos.

38    *poridzesthai*. The verb is related to *poros*, "means" or "resource," and *aporos*, "resourceless" and "perplexed."

39    Socrates's turn from "beautiful" to "good" will eventually lead Meno to agree that everyone desires what seems good.

**Meno:** There are those who believe that bad things help, and there are also those who recognize that they harm.

**Socrates:** And so, do those who believe that bad things help also seem to you to recognize that the bad things are bad?

**Meno:** No, that, at any rate, doesn't seem to me to be the case at all.

E   **Socrates:** Then it's clear that those who fail to recognize them don't desire bad things, but rather desire those things they thought were good, but are in fact bad; so that it's clear that those who fail to recognize these things and think that they're good desire good things. Or don't they?

**Meno:** It does look like they, at least, do.

**Socrates:** What about this? Those who, as you claim, desire bad things while believing that bad things harm those to whom they come, surely recognize that they'll be harmed by them?

78A   **Meno:** That's a necessity.

**Socrates:** But don't these people think that those who are harmed are wretched to the extent that they're being harmed?

**Meno:** This, too, is a necessity.

**Socrates:** And that the wretched are unfortunate?

**Meno:** I, for one, think so.

**Socrates:** Now is there anyone who wants to be wretched and unfortunate?

**Meno:** It doesn't seem so to me, Socrates.

**Socrates:** Therefore, no one, Meno, wants bad things, if in fact no one wants to be such a person. For what else is it to be wretched than to desire bad things—and also to get them?

B   **Meno:** It looks as if what you say is true, Socrates, and no one wants bad things.

**Socrates:** Now weren't you saying a moment ago that virtue is wanting good things and being capable?

**Meno:** Yes, I was saying that.

**Socrates:** So then, in what was said, isn't the wanting present in all people, and in this respect, at least, one person isn't at all better than another?

**Meno:** It appears so.

**Socrates:** But it's clear that if in fact one person is better than another, he'd be superior in terms of being capable.

**Meno:** Certainly.

**Socrates:** Therefore, as it seems, this, according to your account, is
C       virtue: the capacity to provide oneself with good things.[40]

**Meno:** It seems to me to hold entirely as you now take it, Socrates.

**Socrates:** So, let's see whether in this case as well what you're saying
is true; for perhaps there might be something to what you say. You
claim that virtue is being able to provide oneself with good things?

**Meno:** I do indeed.

**Socrates:** And don't you call *good* things like health and also wealth?

**Meno:** I mean getting gold, too, and also silver, and honors in the
city and positions of rule.

**Socrates:** By good you don't mean anything other than things of
that sort?

D       **Meno:** No, but I mean everything of that sort.

**Socrates:** All right, virtue, then, is providing oneself with gold and
silver—so proclaims Meno, the ancestral guest-friend of the
Great King![41] Do you add to this provision, Meno, justly and
piously, or does it make no difference to you, but even if one provides oneself with them unjustly, you call it virtue just the same?

**Meno:** Certainly not, Socrates.

**Socrates:** But you call it vice?

**Meno:** I certainly do, entirely.

**Socrates:** One must therefore, as it seems, attach to this provision jus-
E       tice or moderation or piety, or some other part of virtue; otherwise,
it won't be virtue, even if it succeeds in providing good things.

**Meno:** For how, without these things, could it come to be virtue?

**Socrates:** And *not* to succeed in providing gold and silver, either for
oneself or for another, whenever to do so isn't just—is this lack
of provision[42] not also virtue?

---

40    The upcoming passage is filled with words related to *poros*—"resource" or
      "provision."

41    The Great King is the king of Persia, the most powerful and wealthiest
      ruler of the time. Meno's ancestor, Meno of Pharsalus, together with many
      other leading Thessalians, supported Xerxes during the Persian War. Per-
      haps that is why Socrates refers to Meno as the king's "ancestral guest-
      friend," his *patrikos xenos* (see Bluck, 261).

42    "Lack of provision" is *aporia*—elsewhere translated as "perplexity."
      Socrates has slyly gotten Meno to admit that sometimes being at a loss is
      a good thing.

**Meno:** It appears so.

**Socrates:** Therefore, the provision of such goods as these would be no more virtue than the lack of provision, but rather, as it seems, whatever comes about together with justice will be virtue, whereas whatever comes about without all such things will be vice.

79A

**Meno:** It seems to me to be necessarily as you say.

**Socrates:** Now weren't we claiming a little earlier that each of these—justice and moderation and all such things—was a part of virtue?

**Meno:** Yes.

**Socrates:** Come now, Meno, are you playing a trick on me?

**Meno:** How so, Socrates?

**Socrates:** Because just now, although I required that you not shatter virtue and break it into bits, and gave you models according to which you were required to answer, you neglected this, and are now telling me that virtue is being able to provide oneself with good things together with justice, which you claim is a part of virtue?

B

**Meno:** I am.

**Socrates:** Then it follows from the things you agree to that this is virtue: to do whatever one does with a part of virtue; for you claim that justice is a part of virtue, as is each of these things. Now why exactly do I say this? Because when I require that you speak of virtue as a whole, you fall far short of saying what it is; instead you claim that every action is virtue if it's done with a part of virtue, as if you had said what the whole, virtue, is, and as if by now I'd recognize it even if you broke it up into parts. Now then, as it seems to me, my dear Meno, aren't you required to face the same question again from the beginning—what is virtue?—if every action done with a part of virtue is to be virtue? For this is what's being said, whenever someone says that every action done with justice is virtue. Or doesn't it seem to you that the same question is required again—do you suppose that someone knows what a part of virtue is when he doesn't know virtue itself?

C

**Meno:** It doesn't seem so to me, at least.

D   **Socrates:** For if you also remember, when I answered you a little while ago about shape, we rejected, I suppose, the sort of answer that attempts to answer through things that are still being sought and are not yet agreed upon.

**Meno:** And we were right to reject it, Socrates.

**Socrates:** Well then, best of men, don't think—just don't—that while what virtue is as a whole is still being sought, you'll make virtue clear to anyone by answering through its parts, or make

E     anything else clear by speaking in this same manner. Instead, think that the same question will be required: on the basis of virtue being *what*, do you keep saying what you're saying? Or don't I seem to you to be making sense?

**Meno:** To me, at least, what you say seems correct.

**Socrates:** Well then, answer again from the beginning: what do you claim that virtue is—you and that comrade of yours?

**Meno:** Socrates, I certainly used to hear, before so much as getting

80A     together with you, that you are nothing but perplexed yourself and do nothing but make others perplexed. And now you seem to me, at least, to be bewitching and drugging and utterly subduing me with charms, so that I've become full of perplexity. And you seem to me to be—if I may even make a little joke—most completely similar in looks,[43] as in other ways, to that flat sea-creature, the numbfish.[44] For it makes numb whoever comes near it and touches it, and now you seem to me to have done

B     something like that to me—made me go numb. For I am truly numb in both soul and tongue, and I can't give you an answer. And yet thousands of times I have in fact made a great many speeches about virtue and to many people, and altogether well, as I seemed to myself, at least. But now I can't even say what it is at all. And you seem to me well-advised not to sail away from here and leave your people; for if you did such things as a stranger in another city, you would very likely be hauled off as a wizard.

**Socrates:** You're a rascal,[45] Meno, and you came close to deceiving me.

---

43   *eidos*—earlier used in reference to the intelligible form of virtue (72C). See n13.

44   *narkê*—sometimes translated "torpedo fish," from the Latin *torpedo*, "a state of being sluggish or numb."

45   *panourgos*—a combination of *pan* ("all") and *ergon* ("work" or "deed"). A *panourgos* is a do-anything, someone who is unscrupulous. In the present context, Socrates uses the term playfully. But the serious, indeed shocking, implications of the term perfectly fit the historical Meno. According to Xenophon, Meno (a general among the Ten Thousand Greeks, whom

**Meno:** How's that, Socrates?

C   **Socrates:** I recognize why you've made a likeness of me.

**Meno:** Why, indeed, do you think?

**Socrates:** So that I'll make a likeness of you in return. I know this about all beauties, that they delight in having likenesses made of them—since it's to their advantage; for the likenesses of the beautiful are, I think, also beautiful—but I won't make a likeness of you in return. As for me, if the numbfish, by going numb itself, in this way also makes others go numb, I'm like it; but if not, not. For I don't make others unprovided[46] while I am myself well-provided; it's much rather the case that by being myself

D   perplexed I make others perplexed as well. So now, concerning virtue, what it is, I myself don't know; you, however, perhaps at first knew before you made contact with me; now, however, you are similar to one who doesn't know. All the same, I'm willing to investigate this along with you and join you in searching for what in the world it is.

**Meno:** And in what way, Socrates, will you search for that thing about which you don't know at all what it is? For what sort of thing among those you don't know will you set before you as you search?[47] Or even if in the best case you should run right into it, how will you know that this is what you didn't know?[48]

E   **Socrates:** I understand the sort of thing you want to say, Meno. Do you see how contentious this account is that you're spinning,[49] that it's not therefore possible for a human being to search for either what he knows or what he doesn't know? For he'd search

---

he betrayed) was "clearly desirous of excessive wealth, and desirous of ruling so that he might get more wealth, and desirous of being honored in order that he might increase his gains. . . . For the accomplishing of the objects of his desire, he thought the shortest path was by way of perjury, lying, and deceiving" (*Anabasis* 2.6). Xenophon further reports that Meno counted among the uneducated anyone who was not a *panourgos*.

46   *aporos*—also, "perplexed," as in the clause that immediately follows.

47   Meno echoes (and appears to blur) Socrates's distinction between *what* something is and *what sort* of thing it is (71B).

48   Meno attempts to get back at Socrates by numbing him in return. As we soon hear, Meno is enamored with the clever ring of this paradox, which he no doubt learned from Gorgias.

49   *katageis.* The verb has a range of meanings, including "lead" or "carry down" (especially to the seacoast), "draw out" or "spin," and "bring down."

neither for what he knows—since he knows it, and in such a case there's no need at all of a search—nor for what he doesn't know—since he doesn't even know what he's to search for.

81A  **Meno:** Doesn't this account seem to you to be beautifully put, Socrates?

**Socrates:** Not to *me*.

**Meno:** Can you tell me in what way?

**Socrates:** I can; for I have heard from both men and women, wise in divine matters[50]—

**Meno:** —saying what account?

**Socrates:** A true one, as it seems to me, and beautiful.

**Meno:** What is it, and who are the ones saying it?

**Socrates:** The ones saying it are among the priests and priestesses,
B  as many as have made it their care to be able to give an account of whatever they undertake; and Pindar also says it, and many other poets, too, as many as are divine. And what they say is this—but look well into whether they seem to you to speak the truth. For they claim that the human soul is deathless, and that at one time she meets her end—the very thing people call dying— and at another is born once again, but she is never destroyed. Indeed, that is why one must live one's life through in the holiest way. For those from whom

> Persephone, for ancient grief, atonement
>
> Accepts, of these to the sun above in the ninth year
>
> She returns the soul[51] again;
C
> From them illustrious kings and men
>
> Swift in strength and greatest in wisdom
>
> Grow; and for the rest of time, heroes undefiled
>
> Are they called among humans.[52]

---

50  Either Socrates pauses here, perhaps in a moment of inward reflection (Klein, 93), or else Meno, impatient to hear the speeches of inspired men and women, interrupts him.

51  Retaining the singular *psychan*. See Bluck, 283.

52  The quotation is probably from Pindar. According to some accounts, the "ancient grief" is that of Persephone for her son Dionysus, who was devoured by the Titans. In revenge, "the child-god's father Zeus blasted the Titans with a thunderbolt, and man, having sprung from the ashes, has within him, as well as something divine, the taint of an original sin

Inasmuch, then, as the soul is deathless and has been born often, and has seen the things here and in Hades—all things, in fact—there is nothing that she has not learned; so that it's not at all surprising that it's possible for her to recollect about virtue and also other things, which very things she had knowl-
D      edge of even before. For inasmuch as all of nature is akin, and the soul has learned all things, nothing at all prevents someone who has recollected only one thing—which, indeed, humans call learning—from discovering for himself all the rest, if he is some-one courageous and doesn't grow weary in the search; for to be searching and learning is therefore wholly recollection. One must not, then, be persuaded by that contentious account; for it would make us lazy, and is sweet to hear for the soft among
E      human beings, while this other account makes us both ready to work and ready to search.[53] Trusting that it's true, I'm willing to search along with you for what virtue is.[54]

**Meno:** Yes, Socrates. But what do you mean by this, that we do not learn but what we call learning is recollection? Can you teach me how this is so?

**Socrates:** Just a little while ago, Meno, I was saying that you're a
82A    rascal, and now you ask if I can teach you—I, who claim that there is no teaching, but only recollection—so that it might immediately become apparent that I was contradicting myself.

**Meno:** No, by Zeus, Socrates, I wasn't speaking with a view to that, but by force of habit.[55] But if somehow you can show that it is as you say, then show it.

**Socrates:** It certainly isn't easy; but nevertheless, I'm willing to
B      make the effort for your sake. But summon one of these many

---

for which he must make atonement to the bereaved mother Persephone'" (Bluck, 278).

53   Socrates's rousing call to inquiry combines intellectual engagement (the search for truth) with excellence of character or ethical virtue, in particular the virtue of courage. The sustained effort involved in recollection is good for the whole soul, for our very humanity.

54   The precise meaning of the myth of recollection is unclear. Overall Socrates seems to be trying to persuade Meno, through the power of myth, that there is an eternal, deathless order of things, with which the soul, herself deathless, has a timeless bond. For a non-mythic account of recollection, see *Phaedo*, 72E ff.

55   This is the third reference to Meno as a creature of habit (*ethos*). The first two were at 70B–C and 76D.

attendants of yours here,[56] whomever you want, so that I may exhibit it to you in him.[57]

**Meno:** By all means. You, come over here!

**Socrates:** He's a Greek, I assume, and speaks Greek?

**Meno:** Absolutely, by all means—in fact, born in the household.

**Socrates:** Now pay attention to which of the two ways he appears to you, whether he is recollecting, or learning from me.

**Meno:** I *will* pay attention.

[*Socrates now addresses the boy.*]

**Socrates:** Tell me, my boy,[58] do you recognize that a square area is this sort of thing?

[*Socrates draws a square in the sand.*]

**Boy:** I do.

C   **Socrates:** Now is a square area something that has all these lines— which are four—equal [ABCD]?[59]

**Boy:** By all means.

**Socrates:** Doesn't it also have these lines through the middle equal [EF, GH]?

---

56   Throughout the dialogue, Socrates calls attention to Meno's bond with many-ness: many instances of virtue, many kinds of virtues, many speeches about virtue, many pieces of gold and silver, and here, Meno's many attendants.

57   *en toutôi.* If Meno is to benefit from this display, he will have to do more than attend to speeches. He will have to focus on what happens *in* the slave-boy—on the movement of the boy's soul in his act of learning. What follows, then, is as much a test of Meno as it is of the boy.

58   *ô pai.* The *ô* in Greek signals the polite form of address. It is absent, for instance, when Eucleides in the *Theaetetus* tells a slave: "Take the book, boy, and read" (143C). A *pais* can be a slave, a boy, or a child. (Socrates had addressed Meno as the *pais* of Alexidemus at 76E.) The age of this *pais* is unclear, though he may well be fairly young. He is never called a *doulos*, the standard Greek word for "slave," which appeared in Meno's list at 71E–72A. Socrates's address is here rendered "my boy" to suggest Socrates's courteous, paternal-like manner toward him.

59   Socrates does not mention that a square must be right-angled as well as equi-lateral (cf. Euclid, *Elements*, bk. 1, def. 22). He also makes no use of letters, which have been added here for the reader's convenience, but instead relies on pointing and on the boy's ability to recognize visual images. The reader would do well to ask why, in order to illustrate learning as recollection, Socrates invokes (a) mathematics, (b) geometry rather than arithmetic, (c) a construction rather than the demonstration of a property, and (d) the doubling of a square, a problem not soluble in terms of an articulable side. See n62.

**Boy:** Yes.

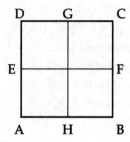

**Socrates:** Now couldn't such an area be greater or smaller?

**Boy:** By all means.

**Socrates:** If, then, this side should be two feet and this two feet, how many feet would the whole thing be? Look at it this way. If in this direction it were two feet [AB] and in this direction only one foot [AE], isn't it the case that the area [ABFE] would be once two feet?[60]

D   **Boy:** Yes.

**Socrates:** But since it is also two feet in this direction [AD], isn't it the case that it comes to be twice two?

**Boy:** It does come to be that.

**Socrates:** Therefore, it comes to be twice two feet?

**Boy:** Yes.

**Socrates:** Then how many are twice two feet? Tell me, once you've calculated it.

**Boy:** Four, Socrates.

**Socrates:** Then couldn't there come to be another area, double this one but of the same sort,[61] having all its lines equal, just as this one does?

**Boy:** Yes.

---

60    In the Greek, no distinction is made between "feet" and "square feet."

61    Socrates hints at the similarity of all squares. Two rectilinear figures are said to be similar (*homoia*) when their angles taken respectively are equal and their sides about the equal angles are proportional (see Euclid, *Elements*, bk. 6, def. 1). Similarity will be suggested more strongly at 87A. It is the most potent characteristic of Euclidean geometry.

**Socrates:** Then how many feet will it be?

**Boy:** Eight.

E   **Socrates:** Come then, try to tell me of what extent[62] each line of that area will be. For the line of this one is two feet, but what is the line of that double one?[63]

**Boy:** It's quite clear, Socrates, that it will be double.

**Socrates:** Do you see, Meno, that I'm teaching him nothing but asking him everything? And now he thinks he knows what sort of line it is, from which the eight-foot area will come to be. Or doesn't it seem so to you?

**Meno:** It does to me.

**Socrates:** Does he know, then?

**Meno:** Certainly not.

**Socrates:** But he *thinks*, at any rate, that it's from the double line?

**Meno:** Yes.

**Socrates:** Now observe him recollecting in order, as one must recollect.[64] [*Socrates now turns back to the boy.*]

83A       But tell me: You claim that the double area comes to be from the double line? I mean this sort of thing: let it be not long on one side while short on the other, but equal on all sides, just as this one here is, but *double* this—an eight-foot area. Now see whether it still seems to you that it will be from the double line.

**Boy:** It does to me.

---

62   Socrates here introduces the word *pêlikê*, "how much." It appears again at 83E and 85A. The word refers mostly to continuous, as opposed to discrete, magnitudes or numbers (assemblages of units) and thus can apply to lines that are incommensurable—in other words, lines that do not have to one another the ratio of a number to a number. The double square will be constructed on just such a line.

63   By stressing "two" and "double," Socrates subtly nudges the boy to double the line. The error will turn out to be fruitful, since it will play a key role in constructing the double square. Throughout this episode, the reader is called upon to pay close attention to how the boy's errors and perplexity contribute to his learning, and how falsehood is integral to the search for truth.

64   Socrates's emphasis on recollecting *in order* (*ephexês*) recalls the crucial claim we heard in the myth—that "all of nature is akin" (81D). To recollect is not to get the right answer to a question but to follow the natural interconnectedness of things.

**Socrates:** Then doesn't this line come to be double that one, when we add another of the same length right here? [*Socrates extends AB to J.*]

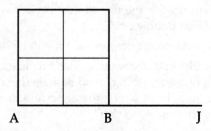

A          B          J

**Boy:** By all means.

**Socrates:** So the eight-foot area, you claim, will be from this line [AJ], if there come to be four lines this long.

B   **Boy:** Yes.

**Socrates:** Now from this line [AJ], let's fill out the drawing with four equal lines. Surely this one here would be what you claim is the eight-foot area?

**Boy:** By all means.

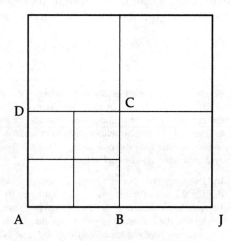

A          B          J

**Socrates:** Then aren't there within it these four areas here, each of which is equal to this four-foot one [ABCD]?

**Boy:** Yes.

**Socrates:** Then how big has it come to be? Isn't it four times as big?

**Boy:** Of course.

**Socrates:** Then is four times as much *double*?

**Boy:** By Zeus, no!

**Socrates:** But what multiple is it?

**Boy:** Quadruple.

C   **Socrates:** Therefore, from the double line, my boy, there comes to be not the double area but the quadruple.

**Boy:** What you say is true.

**Socrates:** For four times four is sixteen. Isn't it?

**Boy:** Yes.

**Socrates:** And the eight-foot area is from what sort of line? Isn't the area from *this* line [AJ] quadruple?

**Boy:** So I claim.

**Socrates:** And this four-foot area is from this half-line here [AB]?

**Boy:** Yes.

**Socrates:** Well then, and isn't the eight-foot area double this one and half of that?[65] So won't it be from a line greater than
D   one this long [AB] but less than one that long [AJ]?[66] Or won't it?

**Boy:** It does seem like that to me.

**Socrates:** Beautiful. For whatever seems so to you, keep giving that as your answer. So tell me: wasn't this line two feet long [AB], and that one four [AJ]?

**Boy:** Yes.

**Socrates:** The line of the eight-foot area must therefore be greater than this two-foot line, but less than the four-foot line.

**Boy:** It must.

---

65   Some modern editors, including Burnet, here insert an affirmative answer by the *pais*, but the addition is not supported by the manuscripts.

66   Socrates's follow-up question seems designed to tempt the boy to make the (false) claim that the desired length must be the number of feet *between* two and four. Once the three-foot line fails, the boy will be out of possible unit-additions to the side of the original square. He will signal his perplexity, the knowledge of his ignorance, with an oath (84A). See n63.

E **Socrates:** So try to tell me of what extent you claim it is.

**Boy:** Three feet.

**Socrates:** Then if in fact the line is to be three feet, won't we attach half of this [AB], and it will be a three-foot line [AK]? For here there are two feet [AB], here one [BK]; and in this direction similarly, here there are two feet [AD], here one [DL]. And so there comes to be this area you're making a claim about.

**Boy:** Yes.

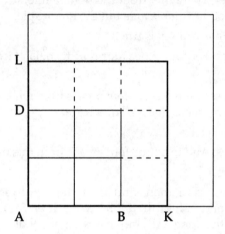

**Socrates:** When it is three feet this way [AK] and three feet that [AL], doesn't the whole area come to be three times three feet?

**Boy:** So it appears.

**Socrates:** And three times three are how many feet?

**Boy:** Nine.

**Socrates:** And how many feet did the double area have to be?

**Boy:** Eight.

**Socrates:** Therefore, the eight-foot area doesn't yet come to be—not from the three-foot line, either.

**Boy:** Certainly not.

84A **Socrates:** But from what sort of line? Try to tell us precisely; and if you don't want to count, just show from what sort of line.

**Boy:** But, by Zeus, Socrates, I really don't know![67]

---

67  The boy utters an oath twice, here and at 83C. Both instances underscore his genuine realization, perplexity, and involvement in the problem at hand.

**Socrates:** Again, Meno, do you realize where he is at this point in his recollecting, as he advances step by step? That at first, he didn't know what the line of the eight-foot area is—just as he still doesn't know even now—but at the time he *thought* he knew it, and boldly went on giving answers as though he knew, and didn't believe he was perplexed; but now, at this point, he believes he is perplexed, and just as he doesn't know, so neither, indeed, does he think he knows.

B

**Meno:** What you say is true.

**Socrates:** Then isn't he now better off regarding the matter he didn't know?

**Meno:** This, too, seems to me to be the case.

**Socrates:** Then in making him be perplexed and numbed, just as the numbfish does, we haven't harmed him in any way, have we?

**Meno:** It doesn't seem so to me, at least.

**Socrates:** In fact, we've done something that, as seems likely, furthers the task of his finding out how things stand. For now, he would even search gladly, since he doesn't know, whereas back then, in an easy-going manner, he thought he could speak well, before many and also on many occasions,[68] about the double area, that it must have the line that's double in length.

C

**Meno:** It does seem likely.

**Socrates:** Then do you think that earlier he would have attempted to search for or learn the thing he thought he knew (although he didn't know), before he fell into perplexity by having come to believe he didn't know, and before he yearned for knowing?

**Meno:** It doesn't seem so to me, Socrates.

**Socrates:** Did he therefore profit from having gone numb?

**Meno:** It seems so to me.

**Socrates:** Now look carefully at what in addition he will discover on the basis of this perplexity by searching along with me, while I do nothing but ask and do not teach. And be on guard in case somewhere you find me teaching and expounding to him rather than asking for his opinions. [*Socrates now turns back to the boy and begins to redraw the quadruple square.*]

D

Now tell me: Isn't this our four-foot area [ABCD]? You understand?

---

68   A humorous echo of Meno's boast at 80B.

**Boy:** I do.

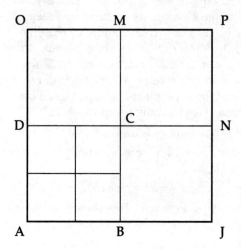

**Socrates:** Could we add right here another, equal to it [BJNC]?

**Boy:** Yes.

**Socrates:** And this third equal to either of these [DCMO]?

**Boy:** Yes.

**Socrates:** Then could we add this one in the corner to fill it out [CNPM]?[69]

**Boy:** By all means.

**Socrates:** Then surely there would come to be these four equal areas here?

E **Boy:** Yes.

**Socrates:** What then? What multiple of this one does this whole area come to be?

**Boy:** Quadruple.

---

69   Socrates had earlier constructed the quadruple square by doubling the side of the original square and completing the figure. Now he builds it block by block. It is clear, especially at this point, that Socrates is doing more than asking the boy questions: he is leading him and has been leading him all along. The slave-boy episode in this way points to something on which the myth of recollection was silent: the role of a guide and helper in the recovery of "past" knowledge. We should note, however, that at each point of the search for the double square, the boy is in fact following the lead of what he himself sees, or thinks he sees, in the diagram and in the logical flow of the argument. In contrast to his master Meno, the boy always gives opinions that are really his own, as Socrates urged him to do at 83C. On the "inner" quality of the boy's answers, see Klein, 104.

**Socrates:** But we needed to get the double—or don't you remember?

**Boy:** Certainly.

85A **Socrates:** Now isn't this a line, going from corner to corner [DB], that cuts each of these areas in two?

**Boy:** Yes.

**Socrates:** Then don't these four equal lines come to be, containing this area right here [DBNM]?

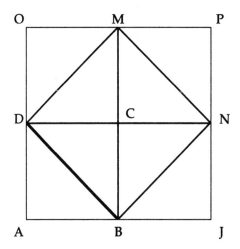

**Boy:** They certainly do come to be.

**Socrates:** Now look closely. What is the extent of this area?

**Boy:** I don't understand.

**Socrates:** Hasn't each line cut off, on the inside, *half* of each of these existing four areas? Or not?

**Boy:** Yes.

**Socrates:** Then how many of this size are present within this area [DBNM]?

**Boy:** Four.

**Socrates:** And how many in this one here [ABCD]?

**Boy:** Two.

**Socrates:** And what is the four of the two?

**Boy:** Double of it.

B **Socrates:** Then how many feet does this one here come to be [DBNM]?

**Boy:** Eight feet.

**Socrates:** From what sort of line?

**Boy:** From this one [DB].

**Socrates:** From the line stretching from corner to corner of the four-foot area?

**Boy:** Yes

**Socrates:** And the sophists call this line "diagonal."[70] So that if the name of this is "diagonal," it would be from the diagonal—as you, boy of Meno,[71] declare—that there would come to be the double area.

**Boy:** Altogether so, Socrates.

**Socrates:** How does it seem to you, Meno? Is there any opinion he gave in answer that wasn't his own?

C **Meno:** No, they were his own.

**Socrates:** And yet he certainly didn't know, as we were claiming a little earlier.

**Meno:** What you say is true.

**Socrates:** But these opinions were certainly present in him—weren't they?

**Meno:** Yes.

**Socrates:** Therefore, in the one who doesn't know, concerning whatever it is he doesn't know, there are present true opinions about those things he doesn't know?

**Meno:** It appears so.

**Socrates:** For now, at any rate, these opinions have been stirred up in him like a dream; but if someone goes on to ask him these same things many times and in many ways, you know that he

---

70 Though the sophists give it a name, the diagonal is *alogon*—without *logos*—in two related senses. One is that its relation to the side cannot be expressed as a ratio or *logos* of whole numbers. Such magnitudes are said to be incommensurable since they lack a common measure. (See Euclid, *Elements*, bk. 10, prop. 7.) The other is that it is without *logos* as speech. The diagonal can be constructed and pointed to but not *said*. To the question "How long is the diagonal?"—that is, "How many units does it contain?"—there is no answer. The sophists are here referred to as knowledgeable in mathematics, as indeed many of them were (notably, Hippias of Elis, who appears in the *Protagoras*).

71 *ô pai Menônos*—an echo of *ô pai Alexidêmou*, "child of Alexidemus," at 76E. The boy is obviously Meno's *pais* in the sense of his slave. But Socrates may also be intending to dignify the boy with a title that typically refers, as it does in Meno's case, to a *free* man's lineage, and at the very moment that the boy has completed a successful act of learning and has been liberated from his false opinions. If the *pais* is regarded as Meno's child—a boy in Meno's household and under Meno's care—then Socrates, by having fostered the boy's learning, has proven to be the better father figure.

D      will end up having a no less precise knowledge about these mat-
       ters than anyone.

**Meno:** That's likely.

**Socrates:** Then without anybody teaching him but only asking
questions, he will have knowledge, himself having taken up the
knowledge out of himself?

**Meno:** Yes.

**Socrates:** But isn't the taking up again of knowledge by oneself
within oneself recollecting?

**Meno:** By all means.

**Socrates:** Then regarding the knowledge he has now, didn't he take
hold of it at some time or always have it?

**Meno:** Yes.

**Socrates:** Then if he always had it, he was also always a knower; and
if he took hold of it at some time, he would not at any rate have
E      taken hold of it in his current lifetime. Or has someone taught
him to do geometry? For he will achieve these same things concerning all geometry, and all the other learnable subjects as well.
Now, is there anyone who has taught him all these things? For
you, I suppose, are just the person to know, especially since he
was born and brought up in your household.

**Meno:** But I know very well that no one ever taught him.

**Socrates:** Yet he has these opinions—doesn't he?

**Meno:** That's apparently a necessity, Socrates.

**Socrates:** If he didn't take hold of them in his current lifetime, isn't
86A     this clear by now, that he had them and had learned them in
some other time?

**Meno:** It appears so.

**Socrates:** Isn't this in fact the time when he wasn't a human being?

**Meno:** Yes.

**Socrates:** If, then, in both the time when he is and the time when
he is not a human being, there are going to be in him true opinions, which become instances of knowledge when aroused by
question-asking—won't his soul for time everlasting be in a condition of having learned? For it's clear that for all time he either
is or is not a human being.[72]

---

72  In the *Phaedo* (73A–B), the character Cebes cites as proof of the deathless
condition of the soul exactly the sort of geometric learning that we witness
in the case of the slave-boy.

**Meno:** It appears so.

B   **Socrates:** Then if the truth about the things that *are* is always in our soul, would the soul be deathless, with the result that you should take heart and attempt to search for and recollect what you happen not to have knowledge about now—that is, what you have not remembered?

**Meno:** You seem to me to speak well, Socrates, I don't know how.

**Socrates:** And so do I to myself, Meno. To be sure, on the other points I made in support of the account I wouldn't altogether confidently insist; but that we'd be better and more courageous and less lazy in thinking that it's necessary to search for what one doesn't know than if we were to think that it's neither possible to find nor necessary to search for what we don't have knowledge about—for this I would in all earnestness do battle, so far as I'm able, in both word and deed.

**Meno:** On this, too, at least, you seem to me to speak well, Socrates.

**Socrates:** Since we are of one mind that one must search for what one doesn't know, do you want us, then, to attempt to search in common for what in the world virtue is?

**Meno:** By all means. Nevertheless, Socrates, for my part I would most gladly investigate and hear about that thing I was asking at first—whether one must take it on as being something teach-able, or as by nature, or in whatever other way virtue comes to human beings.[73]

**Socrates:** If I ruled not only myself but you, too, Meno, we wouldn't investigate whether virtue is something teachable or not teachable earlier, before we first searched for what it itself is. But since you don't even attempt to rule yourself, no doubt so that you may be free, yet attempt to rule me and do rule me, I shall yield to you—for what am I to do? It seems, then, we must investigate *what sort* of thing that thing is, which we don't yet know *what* it is. Now if you won't do more, for my sake, relax your rule, at least a little bit, and yield to our investigating

C

D

E

---

73   Meno leaves out *askêton*, "attainable though practice." It is a telling omis-sion, since practice and exercise in inquiry seem to be exactly what Meno needs (75A). Meno is clearly unwilling to take the slave-boy's act of learn-ing as a model for the inquiry into virtue, in spite of his opinion, which he expresses twice, that Socrates has "spoken well." Unmoved by Socrates's rousing call to action, Meno simply reverts to his former question.

on the basis of a hypothesis[74] whether it's something teachable or however it might be. By "on the basis of a hypothesis" I mean this: just as geometers often do their investigating—when someone asks them, for instance, about an area, whether it's possible in this circle that this area, as a triangle, be inscribed— someone would say: "I don't yet know whether this area is of that sort, but I think I have a certain hypothesis as it were that furthers the task in the matter at hand roughly as follows: If this area is such that when one applies it to its given line,[75] it falls short by the sort of area that is like[76] the very one that has been applied, then one thing seems to me to follow, and another follows if in turn it's impossible for it to undergo this. By using a hypothesis, then, I'm willing to tell you what follows regarding the inscription of this area in the circle, whether it's impossible or not."[77] Now, in this way, too, regarding virtue, since we know neither *what* it is nor *what sort* of thing it is, let us, by

87A

B

---

74   From *hypotithenai*, "to place or set under."

75   Most commentators take this as referring to the diameter of the circle.

76   *hoion*. This word appears, with various meanings, five times in the course of Socrates's speech. Here it hints at the term *homoion*, "similar," as it later appears in Euclid's *Elements*, bk. 6, def. 1. See n61.

77   The problem may be that of inscribing in a given circle a triangle equal to a given rectangle. In the picture below, triangle BDE clearly equals rectangle ABCD. When this rectangle is applied to (laid along) the circle's diameter (the "given line"), it falls short by rectangle CDFG, which is similar to rectangle ABCD, since CD is the mean proportional between BC and CG. See Euclid, *Elements*, bk. 3, 31, and bk. 6, 8, Porism, and Definition 1. Also see n61.

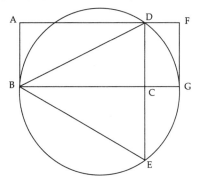

For an exhaustive summary of the interpretations of this disputed passage, see Bluck, 441–61. The reader should bear in mind, however, that the geometric problem is not posed for its own sake but as a model for the inquiry into virtue.

using a hypothesis, investigate whether it's something teachable or not teachable, by speaking as follows: "If virtue is what sort of thing among the things that pertain to the soul, would it be something teachable or not teachable?"[78] Now first and foremost, if it's of a different sort or the same sort as knowledge is, then would it be teachable or not, or, as we were saying just now, recollectable—let it make no difference to us which of the two names we use—but is it something teachable?[79] Or is this, at least, clear to everyone, that a human being is taught nothing other than knowledge?

C

**Meno:** It seems so to me, at any rate.

**Socrates:** And if in fact virtue is some kind of knowledge, it's clear that it would be something teachable.

**Meno:** Of course.

**Socrates:** Therefore, we've gotten free of this quickly: if it's one sort of thing, it's something teachable; but if another, then not.

**Meno:** Entirely so.

**Socrates:** Now the next thing we must investigate, as is likely, is this: whether virtue is knowledge or a different sort of thing than knowledge.

D

**Meno:** It seems to me, at any rate, that this is what must be investigated next.

**Socrates:** Well, what then? Don't we claim that it itself, virtue, is something good, and does this hypothesis stay put[80] for us, that it itself is something good?[81]

---

78   Klein spells out Socrates's analogy as follows: "the given space is (or is not) 'inscribable' into the given circle, *if* the area which is equal to the given space has (or has not) the relation of 'similarity' to another area; excellence is (or is not) 'teachable'—inscribable into the soul, as it were—*if* it has (or has not) the relation of 'similarity' or 'likeness' to something else in the soul" (208).

79   Socrates's offhand reference to recollection reminds us that according to the earlier account there was no such thing as teaching (82A).

80   *menei*—also, "stands firm" or "remains." The verb closely resembles Meno's name. See n5.

81   It is not clear why Socrates applies the term "hypothesis" to this non controversial assumption, which first appeared at 73B–C. Perhaps h intends to bring to light, under the guise of a technical word, somethin; simple that Meno, in his concern for the high-flown and for rule an

**Meno:** By all means.

**Socrates:** Then if there's some good other than and separated from knowledge, perhaps virtue would not be some kind of knowledge; but if there's no good whatsoever that knowledge doesn't encompass, we would, in suspecting that it's some kind of knowledge, suspect correctly.

**Meno:** That is so.

E   **Socrates:** Moreover, it is through virtue that we are good—right?

**Meno:** Yes.

**Socrates:** But if good, then helpful; for all good things are helpful. Aren't they?

**Meno:** Yes.

**Socrates:** And virtue, I suppose, is something helpful?

**Meno:** It's a necessity, based on what's been agreed.

**Socrates:** So, taking them up one by one, let's investigate what sort of things are those that help us. Health, we claim, and strength and beauty and of course wealth—these and things of this sort we say are helpful. Isn't that so?

88A   **Meno:** Yes.

**Socrates:** But these same things, we claim, sometimes also harm. Or do you claim something other than this?

**Meno:** No, just that.

**Socrates:** Now consider: what guides each of these whenever they help us, and what whenever they harm? Isn't it the case that whenever correct use guides, they help, but whenever it doesn't, they harm?

**Meno:** Certainly.

**Socrates:** Now then, let's go on to examine what pertains to the soul as well. Is there something you call moderation and justice and courage and quickness at learning and memory and magnificence and all such things?

B   **Meno:** There is.

**Socrates:** Now consider, among those things, whichever seem to you to be not knowledge but something other than knowledge, whether they sometimes harm, but sometimes help. Take

---

possessions, neglects: the inherent goodness of virtue. For a helpful discussion of this passage, see Klein, 211–12.

courage, for instance, if courage isn't thoughtfulness[82] but instead some sort of boldness. Isn't it the case that whenever a human being is bold without intelligence, he's harmed, but when bold with intelligence, he's helped?

**Meno:** Yes.

**Socrates:** Isn't it the same way in the case of moderation, and quickness at learning, too: the things learned and prepared in the company of intelligence are helpful, but without intelligence are harmful?

**Meno:** Altogether so, absolutely.

C   **Socrates:** To sum up, then, regarding all the soul's undertakings and acts of endurance, when thoughtfulness guides, they end happily, but when thoughtlessness does so, the opposite.

**Meno:** That seems likely.

**Socrates:** If, therefore, virtue is one of the things in the soul, and it's necessary for it to be something helpful, it must itself be thoughtfulness, since all the things that pertain to the soul are, themselves by themselves, neither helpful nor harmful, but
D   when thoughtfulness or thoughtlessness is added, they prove to be harmful or helpful. So according to this account, since virtue is in fact something helpful, it must be some kind of thought-fulness.[83]

**Meno:** It seems so to me, at least.

**Socrates:** Now so, too, for the other things—wealth and such—which we were asserting just now are sometimes good and sometimes harmful: isn't it the case that—just as for the rest of the soul, thoughtfulness, when it guides, made what belongs to

---

82   *phronêsis*. The first appearance of the word in the dialogue. The present passage combines, and seems to identify, knowledge (*epistêmê*), thought-fulness (*phronêsis*), and intelligence (*nous*). *Phronêsis* is Aristotle's term for "practical intelligence" (*Nicomachean Ethics* 6.5).

83   The image of thoughtfulness as something "added" to other goods in the soul recalls Socrates's definition of shape as "that which alone always accompanies color" (see 75B and n19). Thoughtfulness may be said to accompany—or even "shape up"—goods of the soul, including virtue like courage, as their leader and guide. Socrates draws the striking conclusion that virtue *is* thoughtfulness—in other words, that virtue is a kind of knowledge. The present passage should be compared with what Socrates says in the *Phaedo*: "and maybe courage and moderation and justice and true virtue as a whole *are* only when accompanied by thoughtfulness [*meta phronêseôs*]" (69B).

E     the soul helpful, while thoughtlessness made them harmful—so
      in turn the soul, when she uses these things correctly and cor-
      rectly guides, makes them helpful, but when not correctly, then
      harmful?

**Meno:** Certainly.

**Socrates:** But the thoughtful soul guides correctly, while the
thoughtless one does so mistakenly?

**Meno:** That's so.

**Socrates:** So then, is it possible to speak in this way to cover all
cases: for the human being all other things depend on the soul,
89A   while the things of the soul herself depend on thoughtfulness, if
      they are to be good? And by this account the helpful would be
      thoughtfulness; and do we claim that virtue is something help-
      ful?

**Meno:** Entirely so.

**Socrates:** Do we therefore claim that virtue, either the whole of it
altogether or in some part, is thoughtfulness?

**Meno:** It seems to me, Socrates, that what's being said is said well.

**Socrates:** Then if these things are so, good people wouldn't be good
by nature.

**Meno:** It doesn't seem so to me.

B    **Socrates:** No, for then this would no doubt also be the case: if good
     people came to be by nature, there would be for us, I suppose,
     those who recognized among the young the ones good in their
     natures, whom, when they had pointed them out to us, we
     would have taken over and kept under guard in the Acropolis,[84]
     sealing them off much more than our gold bullion, so that no one
     would corrupt them, but when they came of age, they would
     become useful to their cities.

**Meno:** It's indeed very likely, Socrates.

**Socrates:** Then since good people don't become good by nature, is
C    it by learning?

**Meno:** It seems to me necessary by now; it's also clear, Socrates,
that if, according to our hypothesis, virtue is indeed knowledge,
it's teachable.[85]

---

84   Public treasures were kept in temples on the Acropolis.

85   After Socrates's reference to learning, Meno reverts to teaching.

**Socrates:** Perhaps, by Zeus. But what if we hadn't done well in agreeing to this?

**Meno:** Yet it seemed, at least, to be well said just now.

**Socrates:** But it must seem to be well said not only just now but also both now and hereafter, if there's to be something sound in it.

D   **Meno:** So what are you getting at? What do you have in view that bothers you about it and makes you distrust that virtue is knowledge?

**Socrates:** I'll tell you, Meno. As for its being teachable if in fact it's knowledge, I'm not taking that back as not being beautifully said; but that it's knowledge, examine whether my distrust of that seems reasonable to you. For tell me this: if any matter whatsoever, not only virtue, is teachable, isn't it necessary that there be both teachers and learners of it?[86]

**Meno:** It seems so to me, at any rate.

E   **Socrates:** Again, on the contrary, if there were neither teachers nor learners of something, would we beautifully liken it[87] if we likened it to something that wasn't teachable?

**Meno:** That's so. But don't there seem to you to be teachers of virtue?

**Socrates:** Well, very often, although I go searching for whether there might be some teachers of virtue, having done all I can, I'm not able to find any. And yet I search along with many people, at any rate, and especially those who I believe are the most experienced in the matter. In fact, now, Meno, with beautiful timing, Anytus[88] here has sat down next to us; let's give him a
90A   share in our search. And it would be reasonable for us to give him a share: for Anytus here, in the first place, is from a father both wealthy and wise, Anthemion, who became wealthy not by

---

86   Socrates here seems to take advantage of the ambiguity of *didakton*, which can mean either "teachable" or "taught."

87   *eikadzoimen*. The verb *eikadzein* can also mean "conjecture" or "guess" (see 98B).

88   Anytus—democratic leader and one of Socrates's three accusers, the one who was angry with Socrates on behalf of the craftsmen and politicians (*Apology* 23E–24A). He helped restore the democracy after the brief and brutal reign of the Thirty Tyrants (404–403 BCE). The appearance of Anytus is sudden. He probably has not heard the previous conversation but was standing somewhere nearby. In the dialogue, Anytus and Meno never speak with each other.

chance or from someone's gift (like Ismenias the Theban, who's just recently gotten the riches of Polycrates[89]) but by having acquired his wealth by his own wisdom and application;[90] and then, in other respects, too, the opinion of him is that he's not a high-and-mighty citizen, nor a puffed-up and oppressive one,

B   but an orderly and well-mannered[91] man; what's more, he raised and educated this fellow well, in the opinion of the majority of Athenians—at any rate, they keep electing him for the greatest offices. Now it's only just to search with people of this sort for teachers who deal in virtue,[92] whether there are any or not, and who they are. You, then, Anytus, search together with us—with both me and your guest-friend[93] Meno here—for who might be teachers concerning this matter. And look at it this way. If we

C   should want Meno here to become a good doctor, to whom as teachers would we send him? Wouldn't it be to the doctors?

**Anytus:** Of course.

**Socrates:** And if we should want him to be a good shoemaker, then to the shoemakers?[94]

**Anytus:** Yes.

**Socrates:** And similarly, in other cases?

**Anytus:** Of course.

**Socrates:** Now tell me the following about these same things once again: in sending him to the doctors, we claim, we'd be doing a fine job of it if we wanted him to become a doctor. Whenever

D   we say that, do we mean this very thing—that we'd be showing

---

89   Perhaps a reference to the wealthy Athenian Polycrates, who, during the reign of the Thirty, bribed the Theban democratic leader Ismenias to help restore the democracy. See Bluck, 345–47.

90   As we read in Xenophon's *Apology* (bk. 1, 29), Anytus's father was a tanner: he was a self-made man—a true democrat.

91   *eustalês*—literally, "compact" or "trim"; the opposite of *ongkôdês*, or "puffed-up."

92   Our attempt to capture *aretês peri* (the preposition after its noun).

93   This suggests that Meno was staying with Anytus while he was in Athens. Bluck speculates that the family connection between the two men started with Anytus's father and Meno's grandfather, Meno of Pharsalus, who gave aid to Athens during the war with Sparta and was granted Athenian citizenship (349).

94   *tous skytotomous*—literally, "leather-cutters." Possibly a reference to the occupation of Anytus's family. See n90.

good sense in sending him to those who make a claim to the art rather than those who don't, and who exact a fee for this very thing, having declared themselves teachers of anyone who wants to go to them and learn? If we kept these things in view, wouldn't we be doing a fine job of sending?

**Anytus:** Yes.

**Socrates:** Well, don't these same things hold for flute playing and
E   the rest? It's gross unintelligence for people who want to make someone a flute player not to be willing to send him to those who promise to teach the art and exact a fee for this, but who instead make trouble for others in his seeking[95] to learn from those who neither pretend to be teachers, nor do they have a single student of the very subject of study we think worthwhile for whomever we're sending to learn from them. Doesn't this seem to you to be gross folly?

**Anytus:** By Zeus, it does seem to me to be that, and stupidity, too!

91A   **Socrates:** Beautifully put. Well then, it's now possible for you to deliberate along with me concerning this guest-friend of yours, Meno here. For he's been saying to me for some time, Anytus, that he desires that wisdom and virtue by which[96] human beings manage[97] their households and cities in fine fashion and take care of their parents, and know how to take in and send off citizens and guest-friends in a way worthy of a good man.[98] With
B   respect to this virtue, then, consider to whom, in sending him, we would send him correctly. Or is it perfectly clear, according to the argument made just now, that we should send him to those who promise to be teachers of virtue and have declared themselves publicly available to any of the Greeks wanting to learn, and who have fixed a fee for this and exact it?

---

95   Some editors delete the admittedly awkward phrase translated here as "in his seeking to learn from those." See Bluck, 351.

96   The relative pronoun is singular, as if to suggest that wisdom and virtue are one thing.

97   *dioikousi.* See n15.

98   Two things are to be noted in this passage: (1) Socrates interprets Meno's opening question as practical, as if Meno genuinely wanted to know how to become virtuous, and (2) it recalls Meno's understanding of virtue as the effective rule and management of city and household (71E–72A, 73C–D). For the remainder of the dialogue, virtue will be confined to political virtue—the virtue of ruling others, rather than ruling oneself.

**Anytus:** And who do you say these are, Socrates?

**Socrates:** No doubt you, too,[99] know that these are the ones people call sophists.

C **Anytus:** By Heracles, Socrates, watch what you say! May such madness seize no one of my household or of my friends, whether fellow-citizen or guest-friend, so that he's maimed by going to these people! For it's evident that they are the maiming and corruption of those who keep company with them.

**Socrates:** What do you mean, Anytus? Are these people therefore alone so different from the rest of those who make a claim to have knowledge of how to produce so great a good that they not only do not improve whatever one hands over to them,
D as do the rest, but even do the opposite—corrupt it? And they think they're entitled to exact money openly for this? Well then, I'm not sure how I can believe you. For I know that one man, Protagoras,[100] earned more money from this wisdom than Phidias[101]—who obviously produced such beautiful works— together with ten other sculptors. And yet, what a monstrous thing you are uttering, if those who work on old sandals and repair cloaks wouldn't for thirty days be able to escape notice
E returning cloaks and sandals in worse shape than they received them, but if they were to do such things, they'd probably die of hunger; whereas Protagoras escaped the notice of the whole of Greece, corrupting those who kept company with him and sending them off in worse shape than he received them, for more than forty years!—for I think he died at nearly seventy years old, being engaged in the art for forty—and in all this time, down to this very day, he hasn't ceased one bit to be well thought of, and
92A not only Protagoras, but also a great many others, some who came before him, and others who are still around even now. So, which of these two things are we to say, then, according to your account: that they deceived and maimed the young knowingly, or that they have escaped even their own notice in doing so?

---

99  Or, "even you."

100  Protagoras of Abdera, famous for his dictum "Man is the measure of all things." Socrates criticizes this teaching at length in the *Theaetetus* (152A ff.). In the dialogue named after him, Protagoras and Socrates discuss whether political virtue is teachable.

101  Celebrated Athenian sculptor (and friend of Pericles), whose works adorned the Parthenon.

And are we to judge them to be that crazy—those who some claim are the wisest of human beings?

**Anytus:** They're very far from being crazy, Socrates, but much more so are those among the young who give them money; and still more than these, the ones who turn them over to them, the relatives; but craziest of all by far are the cities that allow them to come in and don't drive them out, whether some stranger attempts to do some such thing or a fellow-citizen.

B

**Socrates:** Has one of the sophists done you an injustice, Anytus, or why are you so hard on them?

**Anytus:** No indeed, by Zeus—I, for one, have never, ever, kept company with a single one of them, nor would I let anyone else of my people do so, not a single one!

**Socrates:** Then you're altogether without experience of these men?

**Anytus:** And indeed, may I continue to be!

C

**Socrates:** How, then, you genius,[102] would you know about this matter, whether it has in itself something good or something worthless—a matter in which you are altogether without experience?

**Anytus:** Easily. At any rate, I know who they are, whether I'm in fact without experience of them or not.

**Socrates:** Perhaps you're a prophet, Anytus, since I can't help but wonder, on the basis of what you yourself say, how else you know about these things. But we're not on a search for who those people are to whom Meno would go and become depraved—for let them be, if you want, the sophists; instead, just tell us, and do this hereditary comrade[103] here a good deed by telling him who those are to whom he should go in so great a city, so that he might become noteworthy with respect to the virtue I went through just now.

D

**Anytus:** Why haven't you told him?

**Socrates:** Well, I did say who I thought were teachers of these things, but as it happens I'm not making sense, as you claim, and perhaps there's something in what you say. But now, in your

E

---

102  *daimonie*—literally, "demonic one." Socrates himself claimed to have a *daimonion*, a guiding spirit or genius, that warned him against doing certain things, like embarking on a career in politics (*Apology* 31D).

103  See n93.

turn, tell him to whom among the Athenians he should go. Say the name of anyone you want.

**Anytus:** Why does he need to hear the name of one person? For take any of the fine and good[104] Athenians he might run into—there's not one who won't make him better than the sophists will, if only he's willing to obey.

**Socrates:** And did these fine and good ones get that way spontaneously, and although they've learned from nobody are nevertheless able to teach others what they themselves didn't learn?

93A

**Anytus:** I, for one, expect that they, too, learned from those who came before them, the ones who were fine and good. Or don't there seem to you to have been many good men in this city?

**Socrates:** To me, at any rate, Anytus, there also seem to be men here who are good at political matters, and that there have been men no less good than the ones around now. But have they also been good teachers of their own virtue? For this is what our discussion happens to be about: not whether or not there are good men here, nor whether there have been such men in former times, but whether virtue is something teachable. That's what we've been investigating for a while now. By investigating this, we are investigating the following: whether the good men among those both now and in former times also had knowledge of how to pass on to another that virtue in which they themselves were good, or whether this is not something to be passed on to a human being nor received by one person from another. This is what we've been searching for, Meno and I, for a while now. Look at it this way, on the basis of your own account: wouldn't you claim that Themistocles was a good man?[105]

B

C

**Anytus:** I would indeed, he above all men.

---

104   The term "fine and good," *kaloi k'agathoi* (sometimes translated "gentlemen"), was originally applied to those who displayed the qualities expected of the aristocracy. Later it came to have a broader meaning. Anytus, a man of the people, here uses the term in reference to those who are generally regarded as virtuous.

105   Gifted Athenian statesman who greatly expanded the sea power of Athens. He was largely responsible for the victory over the Persian fleet at the battle of Salamis. In the *Gorgias*, Themistocles is listed among the political leaders who made the citizens under their care worse rather than better, wild rather than orderly. Socrates cites the exile of Themistocles by the Athenians (516D–E). On what "good" means in this context, see n98.

**Socrates:** And that if anyone, then, ever was a teacher of his own virtue, that man was?

**Anytus:** I, for one, think so—if, that is, he wanted to be.

**Socrates:** But, do you think, he wouldn't have wanted certain others to become fine and good, and no doubt especially his own son?[106] Or do you think he begrudged him this and purposely D didn't pass on the virtue in which he himself was good? Or haven't you heard that Themistocles had his son, Cleophantus, taught to be a good horseman? At any rate, he could stay put on horses while standing upright! And he used to hurl javelins from horses while in an upright position; and he accomplished many other amazing things in which that fellow had him educated and made him wise—all those things that were dependent on good teachers. Or haven't you heard all this from your elders?

**Anytus:** I've heard.

**Socrates:** No one, therefore, could have accused his son's nature, at least, of being bad.

E **Anytus:** Perhaps not.

**Socrates:** But what about this? Have you ever heard from anyone, whether young or old, that Cleophantus, son of Themistocles, turned out to be a man good and wise in the very respects in which his father was?

**Anytus:** Surely not.[107]

**Socrates:** Then do we think he wanted to educate his own son in those other things while making him no better than his neighbors in the wisdom in which he himself was wise, if indeed virtue was something teachable?

**Anytus:** Probably not, by Zeus!

---

106  The father-son relation here emerges as a major theme of the dialogue. It appeared earlier, as if by anticipation, when Socrates made much of the virtue and good reputation of Anytus's father (90A–B). Xenophon reports that Anytus neglected the education of his son, who became a drunkard (*Apology* bk. 1, 29–32). Recall that Socrates had played the role of father to Meno's slave-boy when he took momentary charge of the boy's education (see n58 and n71)—not by passing on or transmitting knowledge to the boy but by bringing out what was already in the boy's soul.

107  Cleophantus was reputed to have been spoiled by his parents (see Bluck 370).

**Socrates:** Well, there's some teacher of virtue for you—he who you, too, agree is among the best[108] of those who came before. But now let's look at someone else, Aristides, the son of Lysimachus.[109] Or don't you agree that this person was good?

94A

**Anytus:** I do, in every way and without a doubt.

**Socrates:** Well, he, too, did the finest job among the Athenians of educating his own son, Lysimachus, in all things that were dependent on teachers. But does he seem to you to have made him a man better than anyone else? For you've no doubt kept company with him, and you see what he's like.[110] But if you want, take Pericles,[111] a man so magnificently wise. Do you know that he raised two sons, Paralus and Xanthippus?[112]

B

**Anytus:** I do.

**Socrates:** In fact, as you also know, he taught them to be horsemen in no way inferior to any of the Athenians, and educated them to be in no way inferior to anyone in all that depends on skill, in music and gymnastics and the rest. But did he not therefore want to make them good men? It seems to me he did want to, yet this may not be something teachable. And just so you won't think that only a few of the Athenians, and the paltriest,[113] have lacked ability in this matter, reflect that Thucydides,[114] in turn,

C

---

108   *en tois ariston*—an Attic idiom, probably from phrases in which the superlative is repeated, in this case, *en tois aristois ariston* (Thompson, 198). We would say "among the best of the best."

109   Aristides, Athenian statesman known as "the Just." In the *Gorgias*, Socrates cites him as a rare example of someone who was not corrupted by political power and was held in high esteem throughout Greece (526B). His son Lysimachus appears in Plato's *Laches*.

110   Lysimachus lived an obscure life after receiving land in Euboea and money in recognition of his father's service to Athens (Bluck, 373).

111   The famous Athenian statesman who guided (in effect, ruled) Athens in the early part of the war with Sparta. In the *Gorgias*, Socrates judges him harshly for having corrupted the Athenians (515D ff.).

112   In the *Protagoras*, they are among the "troops" that carefully follow Protagoras as he marches up and down while speaking (315A). In the *Alcibiades I*, the two sons of Pericles are called "foolish" (118E).

113   As if the previous examples were paltry!

114   Not the historian, but the Athenian statesman and "aristocrat of unblemished respectability" (Thompson, 199). Socrates's foursome consists of two pairs of political rivals, a populist and an aristocrat: Themistocles and Aristides, and Pericles and Thucydides. Thucydides is "the example *par*

raised two sons, Melesias[115] and Stephanus, and he educated them well in other respects, and in particular they were the finest at wrestling among the Athenians—for he handed over one to Xanthius and the other to Eudorus; no doubt these seemed, among those who lived back then, to be the finest at wrestling—or don't you remember?

**Anytus:** I do, from hearsay.

**Socrates:** Then isn't it clear that he would never have taught his own boys these things, where teaching required lavish spending, but not have taught them those things where no expenditure at all was required to make them good men, if this was something teachable? Or perhaps Thucydides was a paltry sort and didn't have the greatest number of friends among the Athenians and their allies? Yet he belonged to a great house, and had great power in his city and among the rest of the Greeks, so that if this thing was in fact teachable, he would have found out whoever would make his sons good, whether someone among locals or strangers, if he himself didn't have the leisure for this because of his attending to the city. But I fear, my comrade Anytus, that virtue may not be something teachable.

**Anytus:** Socrates, you seem to me to find it easy to speak ill of people. Now then, I would counsel you, if you're willing to obey me, to be careful; since perhaps also in another city it's easy to do people ill rather than do well by them,[116] but it's especially easy in *this* one. But I think you yourself also know this.[117]

D

E

95A

---

*excellence*" of a virtuous political father who failed to give his son an education in political virtue (Bluck, 377).

115 Melesias appears in the *Laches*. He and Lysimachus, the son of Aristides, lament their fathers' neglect of their education and consult two Athenian generals, Nicias and Laches, on the proper education of their own sons (179A–B). Socrates—whose main military achievement was to retreat in good order—leads them in a discussion of courage.

116 Following Bluck in reading *rhaidion*, "easy," as opposed to *rhaion*, "easier" (Burnet), and W. J. Verdenius in reading *ê* as "rather than," as opposed to "or." See Bluck, 385–87, and Verdenius, "Further Notes on Plato's *Meno*" in *Mnemosyne* 17 (1964), 274–75.

117 In the *Apology*, Socrates mentions two occasions on which he had risked prosecution: once under the democracy and again under the Thirty (32A–E). Anytus, at this point, disappears from the conversation, just as abruptly as he had appeared. His parting words to Socrates recall the passage in which Meno warned Socrates not to travel to another land, where he would be hauled off as a wizard (80B).

**Socrates:** Meno, Anytus seems to me to be angry, and I'm not at all surprised. For first, he thinks I'm badmouthing these men, and second, he also believes himself to be one of them. But if he ever comes to recognize what it is to speak badly, he'll stop being angry; but now he's ignorant.[118] As for you, tell me: aren't there also fine and good men in your parts?

**Meno:** Of course.

B **Socrates:** What, then? Are these willing to offer themselves as teachers to the young, and to agree both that there are teachers and that virtue is something teachable?

**Meno:** By Zeus, no, Socrates, but sometimes you might hear from them that it's something teachable and sometimes that it's not.

**Socrates:** Then should we claim that these people, for whom there's no agreement on this very point, are teachers of this matter?

**Meno:** It doesn't seem so to me, Socrates.

**Socrates:** Then what about this? Do these sophists, the very ones who alone profess this, seem to you to be teachers of virtue?

C **Meno:** In fact, Socrates, that's what I especially admire about Gorgias: you'd never hear *him* promising this, but he even laughs at the others whenever he hears them making promises. Instead, he thinks one must make people clever[119] at speaking.

**Socrates:** Therefore, the sophists don't seem to be teachers to you either?[120]

**Meno:** I can't say, Socrates. I'm in the very same condition as the many: sometimes it seems to me that they are, and sometimes that they aren't.

**Socrates:** Do you know that not only to you and the others involved in politics[121] does it seem that this is sometimes a teachable thing

---

118  Another instance in which Socrates (here indirectly) equates virtue with knowledge. If Anytus had knowledge, he would cease to be angry, for he would know that to speak badly means to speak without knowledge of the truth, and hence harmfully. He would know that he himself speaks badly and would turn from anger at Socrates to the attempt to improve himself. But such is not to be.

119  *deinous*—also "wondrous," "terrible," "formidable."

120  That is, in addition to Anytus.

121  Literally, "to the other political men." Meno may in fact be in Athens on a political mission: to enlist the city's help on behalf of his fellow Pharsalian aristocrats, who were threatened by the tyrant Lycophron. See Bluck, 121.

D    and sometimes isn't, but also Theognis, the poet—do you know that he says the very same thing?[122]

**Meno:** In what sort of verses?

**Socrates:** In the elegiacs, where he says

> So by their side do drink and eat, and with them sit
> And pleasing be to them whose might is great.
> For from the good be taught good things, but if

E    > With bad you mix, you'll ruin even what sense you have.

You know that in these lines he speaks of virtue as being something teachable?

**Meno:** It appears so, at least.

**Socrates:** While in *other* lines, shifting his ground a bit, he claims:

> But if intellect could be made and put into a man

—he says something like this—then those who had the power to do this

> Would carry off rewards many and great,

and

> Not ever from a good father would a bad son be born,

96A    > If he heeds sound-minded words. But by teaching

> Not ever will you make the bad man good.

Do you realize that he's contradicting himself concerning the same things?

**Meno:** It appears so.

**Socrates:** Can you tell me,[123] then, of any other matter whatsoever, in which those who allege that they are teachers are not only not agreed to be teachers of others, nor even to have knowledge themselves, but rather are also agreed to be worthless concern-

B    ing the very matter of which they claim to be teachers—while those who are agreed to be themselves fine and good sometimes claim that this very thing is teachable, and sometimes don't? Now would you claim that people who are so confused about anything whatsoever are in a strict sense teachers of it?

**Meno:** By Zeus, I, for one, certainly wouldn't.

---

122  Theognis of Megara, sixth-century lyric poet.

123  Socrates again mimics Meno's opening question (70A).

**Socrates:** Then if neither the sophists nor those who are themselves fine and good are teachers of the matter, is it clear that there wouldn't be others either?

**Meno:** It doesn't seem so to me.

C **Socrates:** But if no teachers, then no learners either?

**Meno:** It seems to me to be just as you say.

**Socrates:** But have we, at least, agreed that a matter of which there are neither teachers nor learners—this would not at all be something teachable?

**Meno:** We've agreed.

**Socrates:** Now of virtue nowhere do there appear to be teachers?

**Meno:** That is so.

**Socrates:** But if no teachers, then no learners either?

**Meno:** So it appears.

**Socrates:** Virtue, therefore, would not be something teachable?

D **Meno:** It seems not, if indeed we've investigated correctly. So that now I'm really wondering whether there even are any good men, or, if they do become good, what might be the way of their coming to be.

**Socrates:** I'm afraid that we, Meno, are pretty paltry men, you and I, and Gorgias hasn't adequately educated you, nor Prodicus me.[124] So, above all else, we must pay attention to ourselves and
E search for whoever will make us better in one way or another. I say this after taking a look at the recent search—how ridiculously it has escaped us that it's not only when knowledge does the guiding that affairs are carried out correctly and well by human beings; perhaps that's why recognizing what in the world the way is in which men become good also keeps fleeing from us.

**Meno:** How do you mean that, Socrates?

97A **Socrates:** In this way: that good men must be helpful—we've correctly agreed that this, at least, could not be otherwise. Is that so?

**Meno:** Yes.

**Socrates:** And that they will in fact be helpful, if in our affairs they guide us correctly—to this, too, I suppose, we did a fine job of agreeing?

**Meno:** Yes.

---

124 On Prodicus, see 75E and n25.

**Socrates:** But that it isn't possible to guide correctly unless one is thoughtful—in this we're like those who haven't correctly agreed.

**Meno:** What exactly do you mean by "correctly"?

**Socrates:** I'll tell you. If a person who knows the road to Larissa (or wherever else you like) should walk there and guide others, no doubt he would guide correctly and well?

**Meno:** Certainly.

B **Socrates:** And what if there's someone who opines correctly which road it is, but has neither gone there nor has knowledge— wouldn't he, too, guide correctly?

**Meno:** Certainly.

**Socrates:** And so long, at any rate, as he somehow has a correct opinion about things of which the other has knowledge, he'll be in no way a worse guide, in supposing what's true but not being thoughtful about it, than the one who is thoughtful about this.

**Meno:** In no way.

**Socrates:** True opinion, therefore, is in no way a worse guide with a view to correctness of action than thoughtfulness;[125] and this is what we left out just now in our investigation regarding what
C sort of thing virtue is, when we said that only thoughtfulness guides acting correctly—there was also true opinion.

**Meno:** That's likely, at least.

**Socrates:** Therefore, correct opinion is something no less helpful than knowledge.

**Meno:** Less so, at least to this extent, Socrates, in that one who has knowledge would always hit the mark, while the one who has correct opinion would sometimes hit it, sometimes not.

**Socrates:** What do you mean by that? Wouldn't he who always has correct opinion always hit the mark, just so long as he opined correctly?

D **Meno:** That appears to me a necessity. So that I wonder, Socrates, if that's the case, why in the world knowledge is so much more honored than correct opinion, and why one of them is one thing and the other is another.

**Socrates:** Do you know why you're wondering, or should I tell you?

**Meno:** By all means, tell me.

---

125  Virtue was defined as thoughtfulness, *phronêsis*, at 88D.

**Socrates:** It's because you haven't paid attention to the statues of Daedalus[126]—but maybe there aren't any in your parts.[127]

**Meno:** And with a view to what exactly are you saying this?

**Socrates:** Because these, too, if they haven't been tied down, slip off and run away, but if they have been tied down, they stay with you.[128]

E    **Meno:** Well, what about it?

**Socrates:** To have acquired one of his productions, when it's been let loose, isn't worth much in value—just like a slave prone to run away—for it doesn't stay with you; but when tied down, it's worth much.[129] For the works are altogether beautiful. Now with a view to what do I say these things? With a view to true opinions. For true opinions, too, for as much time as they stay

98A    with you, are a beautiful thing and accomplish all good things. Yet they're not willing to stay with you for a long time, but they run away out of the human being's soul; as a result, they're not worth much, until someone binds them with a reasoning out of the cause.[130] And this, my comrade Meno, is recollection, as was agreed by us earlier.[131] But when once they're bound, they first

---

126 Daedalus—mythic craftsman who devised the Cretan labyrinth that housed the Minotaur. Among his many wonders were statues so lifelike that they were said to move their eyes and walk around. At *Euthyphro* 11C, Socrates refers to the runaway statues of Daedalus and calls the craftsman his ancestor, no doubt because Socrates's father was also a sculptor of sorts, a stonemason.

127 Probably a dig at the cultural backwardness of Thessaly, the place to which wisdom has supposedly emigrated (70A–B).

128 *paramenei*—the third *menein* verb in the dialogue (*menein*, "stay put," occurred at 87D and *perimenein*, "stay around," at 76E). See n5 on Meno's name. *Paramenein* refers not only to physically staying near but also, in reference to slaves, to remaining faithful. See also 93A: as a result of his excellent education, Cleophantus could "stay put" on horses.

129 Socrates appeals to Meno's love of beautiful possessions (77B).

130 *aitias logismôi*. Socrates seems to be referring to the search in one's thinking for reasons that serve as the stabilizing ground of true opinions. The word for "cause," *aitia*, can also mean "responsibility," "blame," or "guilt."

131 The unexpected return of recollection, here defined in a non-mythic way, is striking, especially since the exploration of the hypothesis that virtue is knowledge was based on the further assumption that knowledge is teachable (see 87C and n79). If recollection is what Socrates says it is in this passage, one wonders in what way the search for the double square was

become instances of knowledge, then steadfast.[132] And that's exactly why knowledge is a thing more honored than correct opinion: knowledge differs from correct opinion by a bond.

**Meno:** By Zeus, Socrates, it *is* something like that!

B   **Socrates:** And yet I, too, speak as one who doesn't know but guesses and makes likenesses.[133] But that correct opinion and knowledge are something different from one another—this I don't at all believe I'm guessing at, but if there's anything else I would claim to know (and I would claim that of few things), then one thing, this very one, I would place among those things that I do know.

**Meno:** And indeed, Socrates, what you say is correct.

**Socrates:** What about this? Isn't it correctly said that true opinion, when it guides the work of each action, accomplishes it in no way worse than knowledge?

**Meno:** Here, too, you seem to me to say what's true.

C   **Socrates:** Correct opinion, therefore, will be in no way worse than knowledge, nor less helpful for actions, nor will the man who has correct opinion than he who has knowledge.

**Meno:** That's so.

**Socrates:** And, moreover, the good man has been agreed by us to be helpful.

**Meno:** Yes.

**Socrates:** Well then, since not only through knowledge would men be good and helpful to cities (if in fact they would be), but also through correct opinion, and since neither of these two
D   belongs to human beings by nature (neither knowledge nor true opinion), since they are acquired[134]—or does it seem to you that either of these two is by nature?

**Meno:** Not to me, at least.

**Socrates:** Then since these are not by nature, neither would the good be so by nature.

**Meno:** Certainly not.

---

a reasoning out of a *cause*. The same question could be asked about the search for what virtue is.

132   *monimoi*—from *menein*, "stay put" or "remain."

133   *eikadzôn*. See n. 87.

134   Reading, with Apelt, *ont' epiktêta* for *out' epiktêta*. For a discussion of this disputed phrase, see Bluck (416–17) and Klein (251n26).

**Socrates:** And since they're not so by nature, we were investigating next whether virtue was something teachable.

**Meno:** Yes.

**Socrates:** Then did it seem to be something teachable, if virtue is thoughtfulness?

**Meno:** Yes.

**Socrates:** And if it were in fact something teachable, it seemed it would be thoughtfulness?

**Meno:** Entirely so.

E **Socrates:** And if indeed there should be teachers, it seemed it would be something teachable, while if there aren't any, it would not be something teachable?

**Meno:** Just so.

**Socrates:** But surely we've agreed that there are no teachers of it.

**Meno:** That's so.

**Socrates:** Have we agreed, therefore, that it's neither something teachable, nor is it thoughtfulness?

**Meno:** Entirely so.

**Socrates:** But surely we agree that it's something good, at any rate?

**Meno:** Yes.

**Socrates:** And that that which guides correctly is helpful and good?

**Meno:** Entirely so.

99A **Socrates:** And that only these things, being two, guide correctly, true opinion and knowledge, which a human being who guides correctly has—for things that come about correctly on the basis of some sort of chance don't come about through human guidance—but what a human being has who is a guide toward what is correct are these two things: true opinion and knowledge.

**Meno:** It seems that way to me.

**Socrates:** Then since it isn't something teachable, does virtue no longer prove to be knowledge either?

**Meno:** It appears not.

B **Socrates:** Of two things, therefore, that are good and helpful, one of the pair has been let go, and knowledge wouldn't be a guide in political action.

**Meno:** It doesn't seem so to me.

**Socrates:** Therefore, it was not by some wisdom, nor by being wise, that men of this sort guided their cities, Themistocles and his ilk, and those whom Anytus here[135] was just mentioning. That's also why they aren't able to make others of the sort they themselves are, inasmuch as they aren't of that sort through knowledge.

**Meno:** It's likely, Socrates, that it is as you say.

**Socrates:** So, if it's not by knowledge, then by good opinion[136] proves to be exactly what's left; it is this that the political men use to set their cities right, in no way differing from soothsayers and divine prophets with respect to being thoughtful.[137] For these, too, when they're inspired, say true things, indeed many, but they know nothing of what they say.[138]

**Meno:** It looks like that's the case.

**Socrates:** Then, Meno, is it befitting to call divine those men who, not having intelligence, get many things right, indeed great ones, in what they do and say?

**Meno:** Entirely so.

**Socrates:** We would therefore correctly call divine those whom we were mentioning just now, soothsayers and prophets and also all those adept at poetry. Those adept at politics, too, not least among these, we would claim are divine and are inspired, since they are breathed upon and possessed by the god, whenever by speaking they should get many matters right, indeed great ones, while knowing nothing of what they say.

**Meno:** Entirely so.

---

135  The phrase (which Socrates repeats at 100B) suggests that Anytus is somewhere nearby, though perhaps not close enough to hear the conversation. After issuing his warning to Socrates (94E–95A), he may have gotten up in a huff and walked away, but did not go far from his guest-friend. As Klein observes, there is something "phantom-like" about the way Anytus appears, vanishes, and then reappears (253).

136  *eudoxia*—from *eu* ("well") and *doxa* ("opinion"). The word means "good repute," "honor," or "glory." Socrates chooses a word that blurs the distinction between the good judgment that political leaders use to guide their cities and the good opinion their fellow citizens have of them. (See Klein, 253–54.) Socrates used the related adjective *eudokimos* in his first response to Meno (70A) and a form of the related verb (*eudokimein*) in reference to Protagoras (91E).

137  The historian Thucydides credits Themistocles, who was just mentioned, with extraordinary gifts of mind and calls him "the most excellent divine [*eikastês*] of things that were to happen in the most distant future" (*History of the Peloponnesian War* bk. 1, 138).

138  These inspired truth tellers differ from Socrates's "priests and priestesses," who make it their care to give an account of whatever they undertake (81A–B). Socrates called Anytus a prophet at 92C.

**Socrates:** No doubt women, at any rate, Meno, also call good men divine; and the Spartans, whenever they celebrate some good man, say, "A godly man is he."

E    **Meno:** They, too, appear, at least, to speak correctly, Socrates. Yet perhaps Anytus here is annoyed with you for saying so.

**Socrates:** That's not at all my concern. We'll converse with him again at another time; but as for now, if in all this discussion we both searched and were speaking in a fine way, then virtue would be neither by nature nor something teachable, but would come to

100A    those to whom it does come by divine lot without intelligence, unless someone should be of the sort among those adept at politics who is also capable of making another adept at politics. But if there should be one of this sort, he could almost be said to be among the living such as what Homer says Tiresias is among the dead, when he says about him that of those in Hades "he alone has his wits about him, while the rest flit about as shades."[139] In the same way, here, too, someone of this sort would be, regarding virtue, just like a true thing[140] next to shadows.

B    **Meno:** You seem to me to speak most beautifully, Socrates.

**Socrates:** Well then, on the basis of this reasoning, Meno, virtue manifests itself to us as coming to whomever it does come by divine lot; but we shall know the clear truth[141] about it only at that time, when, before attempting to search for the way in which virtue comes to human beings, we first attempt to search for what in the world virtue is, itself by itself. But now the hour has come for me to go;[142] as for you, persuade your guest-friend, Anytus here, too, of these very things of which you yourself are persuaded, so that he may be gentler, since, if you should persuade him, it's possible that you will benefit the Athenians as well.

---

139  See *Odyssey* 10, 494–95. Tiresias is the blind Theban prophet who tells Odysseus the stages of his journey and how to make his way home to Ithaca. The *Meno* ends in the Underworld of correct opinion. The descent began when Socrates yielded to Meno and agreed to forego the "What is it?" question in order to inquire into whether virtue is teachable (87B–C).

140  *alêthes pragma.*

141  *to saphes*—literally, "what's clear." The phrase is used in connection with the revelations of oracles and prophets.

142  The ominous words foreshadow Socrates's trial and execution only three years later. Socrates uses the same expression at the end of his speech in the *Apology*, where the next clause is, "I go to die" (42A). Euthyphro, too, uses the expression, as he goes off to prosecute his own father for murder (*Euthyphro* 15E).

# GLOSSARY

**account**, **argument**, or **speech** (*logos*). Noun corresponding to the verb *legein*, which means "say," "speak," "tell" or "assert." *Logos* has a wide range of meanings, including "sentence," "speech," "account," "argument," and even "ratio," all of which can be traced back to the root meaning of *legein*: "gather," "collect" or "select." We translate *logos* as **account**, **argument**, or **speech**, and the related noun *logismos* as **reasoning out**. *Alogia*, the absence of *logos*, we render as **folly**. The related verb, *dia-legesthai* (literally, to talk through), we translate as **converse**.

**being** (*ousia*). Noun derived from the feminine participle of the verb "to be." *Ousia* originally refers to a man's property, especially his immovable property, his "real" estate. In the *Meno*, and elsewhere in the dialogues, it refers to whatever constitutes the core of a given thing, that thing's "substance."

**find** (*heuriskein*). One of several verbs used in the dialogue to characterize the act of intellectual discovery. Related terms are **find out** (*ex-euriskein*) and **discover** (*an-euriskein*).

**intelligence** (*nous*). The most immediate type of intellectual apprehension, whether of objects lofty and remote or of those directly before us. We translate *nous* as **intelligence** (and once as **sense**), *a-noia* as **unintelligence**, and the related verb *en-noein* as **realize**. An idiom involving *nous*— *prosechein ton noun*, literally, apply one's *nous*—we render as **pay attention**. The word *noêma* (which occurs only once) we translate as **intellect**.

**knowledge** (*epistêmê*). *Epistêmê*, in Greek, refers to knowledge in the sense of a comprehensive, articulable understanding of a specific subject matter. We translate the corresponding verb, *epistasthai*, as **have knowledge**.

**know** (*eidenai*). *Eidenai* is the perfective form of the verb "to see," *horan*. To know, then, is to have seen. The related noun, *eidos*, we translate as

**form** or, in one case, **looks** (80A). The *eidos* is the characteristic "look" of a thing, the aspect of it that can be glimpsed only by the mind's eye. See **being** above. *Ousia* and *eidos* are names for the proper object of genuine knowing.

**learn** or **understand** (*manthanein*), **learning** (*mathêsis*), **learner** (*mathêtês*), **stupidity** (*amathia*). *Mathêsis* is the activity of learning. It comes from the verb *manthanein*, which means both "learn" and "understand," and is the origin of our word "mathematics." Mathematics, one might say, is the very model of that which can be learned; hence the slave-boy demonstration here in the *Meno*.

**memory** (*mnêmê*). *Mnêmê*, related to our word "mind," is connected with a number of words that turn up in the dialogue: **remember** (*mimnêskein*), **good at remembering** (*mnêmôn*), and even Meno's name (*Menôn*). But the key memory-related words are **recollect** (*anamimnêskein*) and **recollection** (*anamnêsis*). To recollect is literally to bring to one's mind or memory (*mnêmê*) again (*ana*). (In the active voice, the verb can also mean "remind.") The noun *anamnêsis* (like *mathêsis*, its virtual synonym in the dialogue) refers less to the result of the process of recollection than to the activity itself.

**opinion** (*doxa*). *Doxa* is derived from the verb *dokein*, to seem: a *doxa* is a judgment about what *seems so* to us at a given moment. As such, *doxai* form the ever-changing substrate of Socratic inquiry. Related words that appear in the dialogue are **opine** (*doxazein*), **good opinion** (*eudoxia*), **well thought of** (*eudokimos*), and **be well thought of** (*eudokimein*).

**perplexity** or **lack of provision** (*aporia*), **be perplexed** (*aporein*), **provision** (*poros*), **provide** (*porizesthai*). *Poros* (from *peran*, "to cross, pass through, penetrate") originally referred to a ford or ferry—that is, a way or means of crossing a river. It later comes to refer more generally to a **provision** or means of accomplishing some task. To be without such a means or way, to be *a-poros*, is to lack provision, be at an impasse, **be perplexed**. *Aporia* refers, then, to the condition of **perplexity** or **lack of provision**—or sometimes to the matter or problem that gives rise to that condition.

**recognize** (*gignôskein*). Related to our words "know" and "cognition," *gignôskein* suggests knowledge and judgment born of intimacy and familiarity with persons and things. With one exception (71B5), we translate *gignôskein* as **recognize**.

**search** (*zêtêsis*), **search for** or **seek** (*zêtein*); **look** or **investigate** (*skopein, skeptesthai*). A number of words in the *Meno* are associated with the activity of hunting for or pursuing knowledge. *Skopein* and *skeptesthai* stand out because both are connected with the act of seeing (consider our words "scope" and "skeptic"); depending on context, we translate them as **look**

or **investigate**. But the most important inquiry-related words form a cluster around *zêtêsis*, which refers to an inquiry or **search**. There are over thirty appearances of *zêtêsis* words in the dialogue. They include not only *zêtêsis* and the related verb *zêtein*, but also *zêtêtikos*, **ready to search**, and *su-zêtein*, **join in searching**.

**stranger** or **guest-friend** (*xenos*). *Xenos* means both "guest" and "host"— that is, any of two parties bound by ties of hospitality. More particularly, a *xenos* is someone from a foreign city or land, with whom one is on friendly terms and to whom one owes cordial and respectful treatment.

**thoughtfulness** (*phronêsis*), **thoughtful** (*phronimos, emphrôn*), **be thoughtful** (*phronein*), **thoughtlessness** (*aphrosunê*), **thoughtless** (*aphrôn*). The noun *phronêsis* and the corresponding verb *phronein* can be used to characterize thought or thoughtfulness about a wide range of objects. But in contrast to *epistêmê* and *mathêsis* (see above) and true to their common root, *phrên*—which means "midriff," "chest," "heart"—*phronêsis* and *phronein* primarily refer to **thoughtfulness** or mindfulness about matters of human concern—matters of the heart in the broadest sense.

**virtue** (*aretê*). Although *aretê* is excellence or goodness of any kind, it refers primarily to human excellence. In its earliest appearances, in Homer, it often refers in particular to prowess or valor in war. Like the Greek word *harmonia* (a scale or mode, that is, an assemblage of tones that fit well together), *aretê* may ultimately be derived from the verb *arariskein*, to fit or join together. The suggestion, then, may be that *aretê* is or involves a certain fitness, a developed capacity, to engage well in certain peak activities— perhaps especially those that require steadfastness and courage.

# SELECT BIBLIOGRAPHY

Anastaplo, George, and Lawrence Berns. *Plato's Meno*. Focus Philosophical Library. Indianapolis: Hackett Publishing, 2004.

Bartlett, Robert C. *Plato, "Protagoras" and "Meno."* Ithaca, NY: Cornell University Press, 2004.

Bluck, R. S. *Plato's Meno*. Cambridge: Cambridge University Press, 1961.

Burnet, John. *Platonis Opera*. Vol. 3. Oxford: Clarendon Press, 1903.

Grube, G. M. A. *Plato, Five Dialogues: Euthyphro, Apology, Crito, Meno, Phaedo*. Indianapolis: Hackett Publishing, 2002.

Guthrie, W. K. C. *Meno*. In *Collected Dialogues of Plato*. Edited by Edith Hamilton and Huntington Cairns. Bollingen Series. Princeton: Princeton University Press, 1971.

Klein, Jacob. *A Commentary on Plato's Meno*. Chapel Hill: University of North Carolina Press, 1965.

Lamb, W. R. M., ed. *Plato in Twelve Volumes*. Vol. 2. 1924. Reprint, Loeb Classical Library. Cambridge, MA: Harvard University Press, 1967.

McKirahan, Richard. *Plato's Meno*. Bryn Mawr, PA: Bryn Mawr Greek Commentaries, 1986.

Mollin, Alfred, and Robert Williamson. *An Introduction to Ancient Greek*. 3rd ed. Lantham, MD: University Press of America, 1997.

Schleiermacher, Friedrich. *Platons Werke*. Neuausgabe der zweiten verbesserten Auflage. Berlin (1817–1826). Berlin: Akademie Verlag, 1985.

Stock, St. George. *The Meno of Plato*. 1887. Reprint, Oxford: Clarendon Press, 1935.

Thompson, E. Seymer. *The Meno of Plato*. 1901. Reprint, New York and London: Garland Publishing, 1980.

Verdenius, M. J. "Notes on Plato's Meno." *Mnemosyne* 10 (1957): 289–99.

———. "Further Notes on Plato's Meno." *Mnemosyne* 17 (1964): 261–80.